Human Pin Code

Relationships

ALSO BY DOUGLAS FORBES

Six Six Six

Blu Genes

Seeing is Believing

Echoes of the Universe

Human Pin Code: The Sacred Maths in your Birthdate

Human Pin Code

Relationships

By Douglas Forbes

Enjoy your similarities and
understand your differences

red nolan

ISBN 1 – 86916 – 010 – X

eB&W Publishing SA (PTY) Limited
PO Box 2416, Houghton 2041, Johannesburg, South Africa
Contact: + 27 11 646 4881 or editor@ebnw.com

First printed in South Africa: October 2004

Book Design: Typesetting & Repro Services
Cover Design: Brendan Chidrawi – creativlab
Printing: Mills Litho

Disclaimer

This book is not intended to take the place of professional advice with regard to relationships, nor that the reader necessarily acts upon it. Douglas Forbes is not a trained counsellor or therapist and the advice is given in good faith.

DEDICATION

TO MY MOTHER, IRENE.

Acknowledgements

When I was looking for publishers whilst writing the first Human Pin Code book my friend Dagmar kept pushing me to find this 'woman with a publishing company'. I did in fact find Fiona Coleman (nee Hindmarsh) and of course I had to do her Pin Code to see what type of person she is. As soon as I had done the calculations I knew if anyone was going to make the Human Pin Code a success it had to be her – a dynamic woman with the belief, courage and conviction of what she does. History speaks for itself and it speaks volumes. If I was wrong you wouldn't have seen the first Human Pin Code book, let alone this one. My thanks to Dagmar for pushing me to find her and my special thanks to Fiona for making it all happen.

Something my mother taught me for which I thank her are her values (drummed into me from a very early age) one of which was not to gossip about others. "If you've nothing nice to say, leave it well alone," she'd tell me. "Gossip is as bad as vulgar language – it's negativity you're expressing, which will come back to you". For all your wisdom; thank you Mother.

My thanks to Wendy for her continued support and all the tea she makes for me. To Randolph for his wonderful input into the website and programming. To Leif and Marion for embracing Human Pin Codes so completely and to Alan Ford for his inspiration.

Thanks to all the certified Practitioners for their enthusiasm for the Human Pin Code. And thanks to Lily Deane in Cape Town, Gordon Cowie in Durban, Evy Evambiou in Port Elizabeth and Anne Ekstein in Richard's Bay for their marvellous organisation. Thanks to Nolan Kötting who puts up with me.

Thanks to Martyn and Jayne Southern for their literary support and especially to Jayne for casting her knowledgeable eye over the manuscript.

A big thank you to all the participants, clients, workshop attendees and practitioners. Finally a special thanks to friends, past and present. You helped to shape me, inspire me and teach me, making my work possible.

TABLE OF CONTENTS

FOREWORD

Finally! The next book on the Human Pin Code as promised to us by Douglas. This man can take his place proudly alongside other works and authors who are also presenting humanity with rediscovered knowledge on how to reclaim personal power through using internal technology. The rediscovered texts of the Qumran communities of the Dead Sea present the same picture of man who carries in him all knowledge required to 'heal thyself'. Douglas' mathematical calculations based on Pythagoras's octagon theorem have presented the professional and ordinary layperson with an accurate personal life chart, a scientific window into one's inner worlds.

For most of us, life is at best a gamble and mostly, life gestures us and we do not really have enough knowledge to gesture It. This is where the gift of the Human Pin Code comes into its own. Imagine having your own personal and accurate description of your every strength and potential as well as your recurring 'shot myself in the foot' information at hand, hour-to-hour, day-to-day, year-to-year, and decade-to-decade. The Human Pin Code through Doug's genius, allows you to become the weaver of your own tapestry with personal threads of your own traits, reactive and active.

I can hear you saying, "Oh yeah! Here we go again another quick 30-second miracle cure for all our problems!" That was my initial response. However, I live and work in an environment that allows me to work with large groups of people, giving me the opportunity to evaluate modalities with almost immediate feedback. I am one of the founder members of an African village outside of Johannesburg, South Africa. There are about 400 villagers who have come from the most traumatized background. The majority (around 90%) of the 160 children in the village are victims of sexual abuse, starvation, abandonment, physical abuse, orphaned by AIDS, and are generally operating with crushed hearts. The adults here mostly come from the same traumatised backgrounds who have found themselves grappling with suddenly becoming parents, lovers, and friends with no support other than I have to offer! Well this is where Doug's work has found its niche as a successful tool of empowerment and awareness.

The other end of the spectrum in which I work and counsel from, are members of the public who come from environments that are more privileged. I've discovered that all of us stand on the edge of the same abyss trying to fumble our way through personal changes and relationships. What makes Doug's work so astounding is that it has no limits, making it relevant across language, ethnicity, education, age and class boundaries.

The Human Pin Code is the most powerful instrument for developing relationships. It can replace the protracted period of discovery spent with a friend, partner or colleague with a 10-minute overview and then depending on your needs an in-depth analysis of the person, saving valuable time of fumbling through the hit or miss business before approaching genuine relationship development.

If any of the following questions have been asked by you in the last week, the Human Pin Code is for you: Why me? Is it fair? Why am I acting like a child? Why do I seem to attract the same people into my life? Why do I always react the same way? Why is everything repetitive? Why does everything this year seem to be changing/is horrendous/is full of new beginnings/is sad?

In addition the Human Pin Code will also explain, with reference to yourself and others, why they are always stressed, can never say no, want to take over all the organising, are a neat freak, a slob or dress impeccably, have integrity problems, can't keep their money, look haughty and arrogant but are in fact just very private, don't like fighting, or who are always ready for a fight.

In the Village by using the Human Pin Code we have managed to facilitate our human resource to a level equal to that used by specialists. In addition it warns us of villagers who would be more prone to suicide or substance abuse and which adults or children need gentle treatment. It has also proven to us that the village and individuals receive monies, have accidents, and behave in specific way on certain days, months, weeks and years.

Sounds implausible! Try it and you will discover a human resource tool that is scientific, user friendly and most importantly a reminder that you are potentially as strong as any trauma or joy that you may experience.

Marion Anne Cloete

BA Social Anthropology, Psychophonetics counsellor, trauma and death counsellor, Village designer

INTRODUCTION

I often need to remind myself that what Pin Codes has offered is a 'toolbox' to help us understand ourselves. I cannot stress it enough. Although we think we know ourselves, I have found that 95% of people, who consult with me, understand themselves very little. This is not a judgment, just a fact. But then you may ask, "Who is to blame?" Ourselves? No. I believe, in their infinite wisdom, it is our parents, and their parents, and their parents' parents. Whatever happened in your life they can, and must be forgiven. Our parents and forebears only did what *they* had been taught. I truly believe that they did the best from their understanding. In speaking with many parents, and then their children, the biggest problem is, "my parent/s do not understand me". We call this the generation gap.

In the near distant past, it was expected of us to grow up, marry, and have children. In fact, so much pressure was put on us, that the young 'adults' were encouraged and then lauded when they announced that they were to be engaged to be married. There were very few people who did not marry, after all, 'it was the done and proper thing to do'.

This idea faded somewhat as the seventies approached and 'free' love was available. Couples hooked up, and simply moved in together. The idea of having a baby out of wedlock, (notice the word: WED-LOCK), was tantamount to breaking down the fabric of society. Most religions controlled the ethics and morals of the nation to some degree or other.

There is no doubt that some societal boundaries are a good thing. Where would we be without a belief system? As a member of the human species, we need a hierarchical system; this is the law of nature after all. Within this hierarchy we have created a world that is moving towards increasingly transparency and peace for all.

But still I remind you that in order to reach this state of nirvana, the starting position is our need to understand ourselves. Many people are doing this. By understanding who we really are from the Human Pin Code method, we are beginning to accept themselves. Thus we have begun the process of change. This imbues a true sense of freedom. Forget the idea that "we are all born equal". This statement has caused the human race more grief and confusion than can be imagined. Open up to the possibility that we are more complex than that. We need a benchmark to measure ourselves, in other words, a map of the psychological mind. When we have a platform from which to work, we begin to understand ourselves.

What has this to do with relationships? Almost everything. Before we can have a healthy relationship with another, we need to have a relationship with ourselves first. This self-relationship will prevent us from 'preying' on others for our emotional survival by projecting our needs for fulfillment onto the other.

The human species is the only species that processes with emotions. Incorporated into this process is our fight or flight capacity. This helps us survive. But increasingly, we are beginning to understand that we do not need this, as we have evolved, and as we become more and more 'civilised' we become more civil. Good manners maketh humankind. To be polite invites intellectual intercourse. It shows respect, therefore commands respect, no matter the age difference. No matter who you are, have at least one good set of clothes. Dress up, speak well and you will command respect.

Another important aspect of our relationship with ourselves is that we need to be free from other people's good intentions. We all know the road to hell is paved with good intentions! What I mean by this is, that as we grew up in a society which was governed by rules, our parents did the best job possibly they could, from their perspective. If you are born male, you were expected to behave like a typical boy. If you were born female, you were expected to behave like a typical girl. But for many people it was further from their truth than they could endure. Boy/girl is merely a gender definition and as a classification for determining behaviour, it is discriminating.

The joy of Pin Codes is that it looks at the process and dynamics of the day first, and only then considers gender. It does not infer that there is anything wrong with us; it merely creates the idea that we need to look at what really makes us tick.

The Human Pin Code offers a platform to make that discovery. It has no doubt changed people's perception of themselves, although some skeptics may argue with this. Skeptics have their place – otherwise where would we be if did not have to prove a point. Thanks to them. The only thing that cannot be argued even by the skeptics is cold hard facts. The facts of science are so compelling that we cannot refute their claim. This is why I have chosen to reveal in this book the science behind the Human Pin Code. What science shows is the atomic structure on which all life is based is translated by the Human Pin Code into a language of numbers which interprets our human potential and behaviour exactly. What you are going to read concerning the physics, has never been seen, or published before. It is very simple and easy to understand. Think carefully, long, and hard about it. The possibilities are overwhelming.

When it comes to relationships, they too have a scientific basis, which is revealed by the Synergy Pin Code between the two people. We have relationships for many reasons.

Up until now, we have interacted with other people, on an emotional level, without understanding who they really are. We took one look at a person and the symmetry of that person created what we believed that person to be. Hollywood was fashioned on this notion.

As we grow older, we are expected to behave according to our peer group, our parental guidance and expectation, and integrate into the rules of our tribe (society). But without the basic tools of relationship knowledge, we can become lost. The dominant types conquer their relationships, flirting and seducing all they want, taking what they think is theirs, and move on. Their emotionally crushed partners are left to pick up the pieces of their broken heart. Then the relationship journey begins once again, and the same mistakes are made all over again.

Sometimes we get it right, and we find the 'perfect' partner. Blinded by love causes us to experience a state called bliss. Sometimes even this doesn't last and the next thing we know we're burning black candles at midnight wondering what when wrong. Again! Well I will tell what you what when wrong. You did not understand the rule of engagement. That's what went wrong.

Too many people have been bruised, damaged, hurt or simply left to wilt emotionally. They try and try again, not understanding the rules of the race, the human race. We can minimise the risk. And this is where this book comes in. You can now learn the rules of engagement and the process of friendship, love and all that embraces the dynamics of relationships. Every Synergy Human Pin Code has its rules. Play by those rules and have a wonderful and fulfilling life. You deserve it.

IN THE BEGINNING

The Human Pin Code is a tool we can use to see ourselves and others in a very objective light. It is a non-discriminating science, which does not require knowledge of anything except a person's birth-date and gender. No names, no personal history, no parental or environmental influences. Blind 'tests' have been done in magazines, live on radio and TV and the birth-date that is being analysed, even in a very compressed and, dare I say it, not ideal situation, has had an accuracy that has shocked the reader, listener and viewer. In personal consultations the analysis is very beneficial.

For all its success in the media and with clients I have been constantly asked, "How does it work?" and in this book I will lay out the principles of the science behind the Human Pin Code. It is amazingly simple and for that reason I have chosen to keep it secret for the past few years to protect its use. You can of course, use this book to analyse your own Pin Code and those near and dear to you. However, it is important that the Human Pin Code is used with integrity, as it has the power to uncover the workings of humankind in a way we have never seen before. The establishment of a certification process for professional practitioners has been a critical part of maintaining the integrity and I encourage anyone seeking a professional analysis of their Pin Code to seek only those certified to practise. Details on finding or becoming a practitioner are given at the end of this book.

So often clients have come to me when in a crisis with their love life, career or with their finances. Sometimes all three areas of their life are in crisis. In using the Human Pin Code I am able to assist the person to see where in their life they have missed an important learning milestone and help them understand that by fixing this and learning about their potential, and "hot-buttons", they are able to better

1

manage critical periods. They are also able to better capitalise on the periods of bounty which also come our way. There is a time to sow, a time to reap, a time to laugh and a time to cry. It's all about timing.

The development of the Human Pin Code has continued since the publication of the first book. It is evolving as I discover more aspects to it. The first book, Human Pin Code: The Sacred Maths in your Birthdate sets out in detail the first principles of using the Pin Code. This book will provide second level principles to provide greater depth of analysis.

But with all the advances in the Human Pin Code I am still asked the same questions time and time again: "What about people born on the same day?" and "What about twins?" or "Two people born on the same day but nine years apart have the same Pin Code, are you telling me they are the same?". Additionally people born on the 1st, 10th, 19th or 28th of the same month and same year will have the same Pin Code (we use the Fadic principle in reducing complex numbers to simple numbers by adding the digits together, e.g. for 19; $1 + 9 = 10$, $1 + 0 = 1$ and for 28; $2 + 8 + 10$, $1 + 0 = 1$. More about that will be covered later on).

So how can this work? Does this mean that everyone born on the same day is exactly the same? No, they are not the same. Yes, they do have the same Pin Code, and they have the potential to react and respond to situations in exactly the same way as someone born on the same day as them, but they don't. When a practitioner undertakes an analysis on a Pin Code they will be able to see the potential of that person and, in fact, they will see the potential of all people born on that day: this potential is influenced by the people around them, particularly their parents and siblings in their formative years.

Each number in the Pin Code has the possibility of reacting 'actively' or 'reactively'. Take a person born on the 1st day of a month. They have a One in their personality. They have the potential to be a leader, bright, talkative, creative, jolly, and confident. They also have the potential to be temperamental, aggressive, egotistical and have low self-esteem. How this person expresses their One personality will depend on their influences in the past and the current environment they find themselves in. Their One will also be influenced by the other numbers in their Pin Code.

Two people born, one on the 17th December 1933, the other born 17 March 1960, have exactly the same Pin Code but they are born in different decades. The decade influence (1930s versus 1960s) will have an effect upon the expression of the Pin Code.

A practitioner will also understand the effect of decades and synergies with the important influencing factors on a Pin Code. For someone to be identical to someone else with the same Pin Code, they need to have parents with the same birthdates. The chance of this happening is very remote, except obviously in the case of twins. We have, however, been working with computer analysts to find the coincidences of non-twin identical Pin Codes with identical Pin Codes for both sets of parents.

Twins have the same parents (obviously!), so they have, in principle the same potential parental influences upon them. However, the key thing to understand for twins is how the two of them get on. They have an intense sibling influence which two people who don't know each other won't have. The twins' relationship is the determined by the *synergy* between their Pin Codes. We will learn more about this in the book.

The full depth and breadth of the Human Pin Code may seem complicated and complex – actually it is. It takes time to learn the full complexities of the Human Pin Code and that is why practitioners must be certified. However for the reader, or someone who isn't certified, doing a Pin Code analysis will still have enormous accuracy and provide a benefit for the person whose Pin Code is being analysed. The more you do the better you will become and the more value you will gain. Use the techniques on your own birth date and those close to you. This way you will learn how all the components of the Pin Code mesh into an analysis.

The value of learning to do a Pin Code analysis cannot be underestimated, even as a beginner. In life we all yearn to understand why we are here, what we are meant to do and we yearn for 'The One' with whom to share our lives. We become unsettled and unhappy when the reality of life seems so far from what we desire. It's often at this point we seek help.

Julie came to visit me for an analysis. From her birth date I could see this 46 year old woman had big ideas but absolutely no way of making anything happen. She confirmed to me this was indeed the case across all aspects of her life. When I discussed this with her she burst into tears. With her head in her hands she told me with desperation that she comes up with more ideas that she knows what to do with but she's never able to get going with any one of them. She had tried, and her family and friends have all at some time or other tried to help but she becomes frustrated with the help and drops the idea.

Julie explained to me she came from a very competent and competitive family who were all self-made with strong pioneering spirits of get-up-and-go. She felt a complete failure because she couldn't make anything happen as had her two brothers so successfully. Additionally because she couldn't get anything off the ground her financial situation was becoming perilous. She had reached a point of despair.

Often when we compare ourselves with our siblings or parents and find ourselves to be different, instead of appreciating those differences as strengths in ourselves we see them as weaknesses, things that have to be worked on. In my opinion that attitude is condemning ourselves to a life of misery. Too often we are put into a 'box' at birth – usually it's the pink one for girls and blue one for boys – but sometimes, as in the case of Julie, her box was the 'self-starter'. This cultural conditioning sets us up for great difficulties in later life. Julie, at 46, was still struggling to be this successful 'self-starter'.

I explained to Julie that her Pin Code was not a self-starting Pin Code. She was a very creative woman and her ideas were her natural talent. Her desire to make it happen alone was not her natural talent. No matter how hard she tried she wouldn't succeed. The constant striving for this achievement would end in deeper despondency and, potentially, depression.

The look on Julie's face when I said this to her was one of amazement. It was the first time someone had given her permission NOT to be what was expected of her. Her expectation to do-it-alone had infiltrated her personal relationships as well. She admitted no man had been close to her for years because she had this projected attitude of do-it-alone.

Julie had to learn that her family didn't know "what was best for her", by putting her in the 'self-starter' box. I do not advocate any blame to be laid on any parent or sibling. As an adult we all must take responsibility for ourselves. This includes accepting that what has happened in the past is just that – past. Today is the present so go forward from now.

Julie's challenge is to cast off her family attitudes and to develop her creative talents. She needs to learn to ask for help to make her ideas come to fruition. In doing this she will see their presence in her life as a help rather than a weakness which is the way she currently views someone helping her. By embracing help and trusting that this person or those people will take her ideas forward, it will free up Julie to continue developing her creative skills.

It is so important for each of us to appreciate that our conditioning from our environment doesn't necessarily point us in the right direction. By analysing our Pin Code we give ourselves permission to not be someone we were trained to be and to discover who it is we really are. The key to life is to "know thy self". Once we have that key, we can then use the Human Pin Code Synergy technique to understand how we respond in our relationships and, importantly, in our most intimate love relationship.

The day we are born becomes our template. Our potential is imprinted on us on that day. If anyone has an analysis and does not find it at least 95% accurate I would challenge the correctness of their birth date.

Perhaps you were born a few minutes after 12 midnight but the clock in the delivery suite was slow. Check the Pin Code the day before or after to see if that's a closer fit. Alternatively ask your Mother if she recalls anything that might have happened to put a different date on your birth certificate. Approximately one in 100 people whom I have interviewed have had the wrong birthday. I've even had people who've had their day of birth correct but month incorrect.

A woman who came to me for an analysis was distressed when I described the Synergy between her and her husband. It wasn't right at all. I told her I couldn't massage the Pin Code or the analysis to suit her. If the analysis is wrong it is because either her or her husband's birthday was incorrect. She was so disappointed as she'd waited a long time for an appointment but as she got up to leave she suddenly stopped. "Hang on a minute," she said, "maybe this story has a bearing."

Her husband's father had been tragically killed in an accident when his mother was seven months pregnant. To add to the tragedy his mother died giving birth late in the evening. In the morning the baby was taken to the orphanage. Was it possible the baby's birth was registered as the day he arrived at the orphanage and not the previous night when he was actually born?

I have found that a number of clients born in the early part of last century, born during the first couple hours of the morning, have had their birth day registered as the day before. I wonder how many people remember the 'new day' began with the rising of the sun. All-night radio and television have defined the line of time.

When I did the synergy between this woman and her husband on the day earlier she had a smile from ear to ear. "Yes, that's us!" she exclaimed.

The reason I am so confident about the accuracy of the Human Pin Code is because the formula is grounded in basic physics. In simple terms it operates on the law of atomic structure and I call it the science of the Human Pin Code.

THE SCIENCE OF THE HUMAN PIN CODE

This explanation of the science of the Human Pin Code is not a paper for scientific publication. I intend it to be understood by anyone who is interested in reading about the Human Pin Code. This information is just an introduction, and the scientists or academics that would like further details, should please be patient as there is a scientific publication on the way. For readers, please do not be intimidated, as it is not critical to understand the science to be able to calculate and interpret Pin Codes. It is not necessary to know how a surfboard is designed and constructed to be able to use and enjoy it. You know it works and off you go. But for some readers, it is important to understand where the science comes from to appreciate the difference between the Human Pin Code and other methods that are commonly sought by people to find answers to their questions.

It may seem surprising that the Pin Code closest to your own is not a person born the next day but it is a person born on the same day ONE YEAR earlier or later than you. We will cover the process to calculate the Pin Code from a birthday in the next chapter. In the meantime, here are the Pin Codes for the birthdays I am using to illustrate the science behind the Human Pin Code.

Watch the sequence as we move two days from the 9th September to the 11th September.

The Pin Code for the birthday **9th September 1980** is:

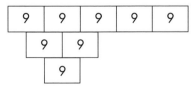

This Pin Code is all Nines.

The Pin Code for the person born the very next day, **10ᵗʰ September 1980**, is:

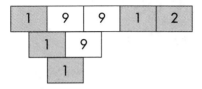

Note that the Pin Code has a One personality (very different from a Nine), and importantly a total of four Ones and a Two and three Nines.

A day later to the birthday of **11ᵗʰ September 1980** and the Pin Code is:

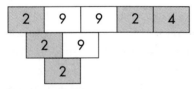

Now we have a total of four Twos, including a Two personality, and a Four and three Nines in the Pin Code. It is a very different Pin Code from the original Pin Code 9ᵗʰ September 1980.

Now look at a Pin Code one month later. The Pin Code for the person born on **9ᵗʰ October 1980** which the same day and in the same year but a month apart from the 9ᵗʰ September 1980 is:

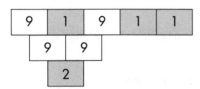

Whilst this Pin Code has the same personality as a person born on the 9ᵗʰ September 1980 the person born a month later in October has a Two as well as three Ones along with four Nines.

We started with a person born on the 9ᵗʰ September 1980. Now lets watch the magic of the progression of the Pin Code unfold before your eyes. You are about to witness the unfolding of the Human Pin Code sequence.

The person born on **9ᵗʰ September 1981** has the Pin Code of:

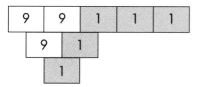

And the person born on **9ᵗʰ September 1982** has a Pin Code where the Nines stay the same and all the Ones change to Twos, like so:

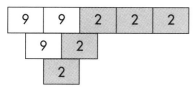

A year on to **9ᵗʰ September 1983** and the Pin Code looks like this:

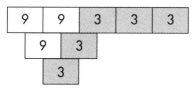

The Pin Code for the **9ᵗʰ September 1984** is:

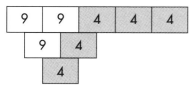

Another year later to the **9ᵗʰ September 1985** and the Pin Code is:

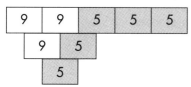

And another year on, **9th September 1986** has the Pin Code:

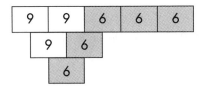

It'll be no surprise by now to know the Pin Code for the **9th September 1987** is:

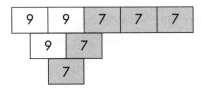

For **9th September 1988** it is:

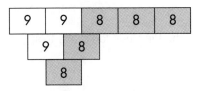

And finally we get to the **9th September 1989**, nine years later from our first birth date of 9th September 1980, and we're back to our origin, except we are in the next decade.

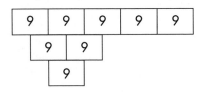

In one decade there are 6574 Pin Code combinations. (365 days in a year and 366 in a leap year multiply by nine years and then multiply the answer by two. We multiply by two as it represents the gender of male and female combination. The calculation is 365 days x 9 years + 2 leap year days in nine years x 2 for male and female influence.)

Your birthday is your blueprint, this is then transported into the Pin Code matrix of eight numbers. Each of these positions represent a facet of our perception, our processing style, each of the facets has choices: reactive and proactive qualities of each number. In fact there are at least 10 proactive and 10 reactive choices for each number so for any one Pin Code there are eight numbers, in other words, we have 1,073,741,824 choices within one Pin Code of how to process **within** that one Pin Code, or seven trillion choices in the entire matrix. This is why no two people are alike.

The principle reveals how the one Pin Code moves year by year. It starts on the day of your birth and then progresses year on year, until the nine-year cycle has been completed. When you know how to calculate your Pin Code, which I will cover in the following chapter, you will be able to check this. You will be able to take your birth day and month and progress the year. Upon completion of every nine years, you will find the Pin Code repeats itself, and is identical to your Pin Code, but notice, the decade has changed.

Spiralling atoms

It is important to understand that I believe that the theory of atomic structure you are about to read has always been here. Just as Galileo believed that the Earth revolved around the Sun, and not as everyone else believed at the time, that the Sun moved around us. Humankind was no longer the centre of the Universe. For this declaration, he was nearly burnt at the stake. An outcry by the people resulted in his life being spared. He died whilst under house arrest.

Imagine looking at the Universe and seeing a new perspective from the point that we might be living inside one atom of a macrocosm. If we can accept this new stance, the Universe is finite and not infinite. We now can compute the size of the Universe. The idea that our planet is actually moving in a spiralling vortex motion, towards our solar system's final destiny, a black hole, becomes a reality, and one we can now prove.

Proof of this can be understood by the appearance of the blue moon. This phenomenon should only happen approximately every 90 years, hence the saying "once in a Blue Moon". We had two in the year 2000, again one in 2004, and the next is in 2012. Take a closer look at our solar system, and the proof is there that we moving in a spiral motion. A journey that our solar system, and the galaxy it forms part of, will end again, in a Big Bang.

The theory, upon which the principle of this spiralling pattern of the Pin Code is based, is the 'construction' and behaviour of a hydrogen atom. Until now, humankind has, to the best of my knowledge, never physically seen the behaviour and most importantly, the construction of the hydrogen atom. Using the basis of Pythagoras' Octagon Theorem, I have identified the construction of the atom. Previously we assumed the electron(s) circumnavigated the nucleus of an atom in a continuous circular manner. This new principle of atomic construction states that the electron of the atom circumnavigates the nucleus, not in a continuous circular motion as previously believed, but is in fact a **spiral action** with a vortex motion.

As the electron descends in an ever decreasing spiral, the centripetal and centrifugal forces create a stress situation as they oppose each other. This ultimately results in a 'big bang' collision of the two opposing forces. The electron then begins to reverse its motion, i.e. reverse vortex, what we have perceived previously is in fact, a 'black hole'. The reverse action creates a vacuum. When the centripetal and centrifugal forces equalise, the process begins all over again. The result is a pulsating effect, and explains why the atoms that where here at the original Big Bang are still here, and why they cannot be destroyed.

The electron begins its journey in an anticlockwise path. In the 'black hole', it follows an anti-clockwise path. Energy is created by the 'release' or force of the big bang, at the atomic level. This action is believed to be the cause of gravity. The vortex action of the electron, also accounts for the drop in temperature as it accelerates towards the big bang. It is for this reason space travel is not an option at present. Think about it: we need gravity to live. We are a 'mini universe' with its black holes. Without these 'black holes', we could not exist. Consequently, without black holes, the Universe would not exist. It is our source of energy.

An atom begins it life at a single point: the centrifugal and centripetal forces make it rotate 144,000 times anti-clockwise following the path determined by the Fibonacci sequence. Mathematician Leonardo Fibonacci, who was born in the 12th Century in Italy, is credited with the identification of this unique series of numbers (1, 1, 2, 3, 5, 8, 13, 21, 34… where adding the last two numbers makes the next number in the sequence, 21 + 34 = 55, 34 + 55 = 89, 89 + 55 = 144, and so on).

Imagine if we could freeze frame by frame, the unfolding miracle of this newly discovered life of the humble hydrogen atom. As we picture the electron, frame by frame on its spiralling journey, we would witness the miracle of life unfolding. Let us look at the results of this, for the secret lies in nature all around us.

For evidence of this, let's take a closer look at the sacred geometry. Sacred just means secret, so let's discover the secret.

A great illustration in nature of this sequence is the Nautilus shell. Its measurements are such that each new spiral grows larger by a rate of **phi**.

Phi is sometimes referred to as the Golden Number. If you divide adjacent numbers in the Fibonacci sequence, for example 55/34, or 610/377, you will get an approximation of phi at 1.618. The reverse division 34/55 or 377/610 gives 0.618. The ratio 1:0.618 is known as the Golden Ratio and is believed to define beauty.[1]

---

1 Eddy Levin, Golden Mean Guage, www.goldenmeanguage.co.uk

Another example of this spiralling action occurring in nature is as a plant grows. From the moment the seedling breaks through the ground's surface, it winds itself up towards the sun in a spiralling sequence. The sequence has the exact proportions of the Fibonacci sequence. The atom's spiralling vortex is expressed in this sequence.

Now you might well say, "What has this got to do with Human Pin Code?" The principle and mathematics of the atom's rotations, of the plant's growth rotation, the Nautilus shell's construction, the solar system and ultimately the Universe, are all based on the same sacred geometry. The whole of life and the Universe's development is based on this movement and it is no different for Human Beings.

We are all in agreement that life in our Universe is based on atomic structure. Air is different from matter only because of the different atomic structure and/or the speed with which the atoms are rotating. When water turns into ice the atomic structure (two hydrogen atoms and one oxygen atom or H_2O) remains the same but the atoms slow down (by reducing the temperature) until ice is formed. Carbon is put under enormous pressure (either within Earth's crust or more recently in huge man-made presses) to form diamonds. It is the same atomic structure; the pressure has slowed the carbon atoms so much they are now one of the hardest substances found in Nature.

However, now that we understand that the atom's electrons aren't rotating infinitely but finitely in a constant spiralling vortex, the pulsating proof of life ('life' to 'death' and back to 'life' again), we can also assume that this is the same for all, including the Universe. This disputes Einstein's theory of relativity, e=mc2 (energy equals mass times the speed of light squared) which implies that the Universe is infinite.

Just as the atoms are 'rotating' toward their 'big bang' so are the galaxies in the Universe. From this perspective, we can surmise that one galaxy is, in turn, one atom of the macrocosm. When you look at a picture of a galaxy, or macrocosm, 'disappearing' into a black hole we are witnessing the same action of one atom of the microcosm. This is identical to the vortex action of an atom on earth inside our solar system, or 'one atom' of the macrocosm. You are beginning to see the macrocosm / microcosm relationship. The difference between one and the other is the speed.

But to prove this, we have to split time and space which I have termed 'Splip' (refer to my publication Blu-Genes, which includes the formulae[2]). It's the speed that's different. Imagine for a moment you are travelling the 1,440 km from Johannesburg to Cape Town, across the amazing Karoo. If you were doing this on foot it would take you 12 days without stopping (but of course a human is unlikely to be able to perform this feat). In a car you can do it in about 14 hours. In a plane it takes you 1 hour and 50 minutes. The space shuttle would fly over the same distance in around 3 minutes. The rotation of the Universe is so incredibly slow from our perspective of time and speed, that we are unable to perceive it even with our current technology. For this reason we can split time and space, where time is relevant only to the space it occupies. If we accept the integrity of our solar system, then our solar system is likened to a 'bubble', along side one thousand million, million, million, million, million other 'bubbles' that comprise the Universe.

We have a common belief that the moon causes the powerful effect of the tides on earth. However, as everything in the Universe, including Earth, rotates, the tidal effect is caused by the Earth's rotations, not by the moon's celestial body, which is only one-sixth of the Earth's mass. The coincidence of full moon and spring tides can be explained by understanding that the rotations of the moon and Earth are in fact closely linked.

This is a new concept that you may need to think about, and your perception may well be challenged with these ideas, as they've not been written about before, to the best of my knowledge.

---

2 An excerpt of which is found at www.humanpincode.com

As all things depend upon the basis of atomic structure, so do we humans. From our perspective, the human body is just a maze of atoms whirling and twirling in space, an apparent chaos. But upon closer inspection, and with a new understanding, it is a microcosmic universe, identical to the macrocosm, our Universe; just look at the stars and galaxies to get an idea as an atomic reference.

Our starting point is our birth date. One of our cycles of nine years 'rotates' through its nine-year span until we return to the end, or the same point where it began. Our birthday, or Pin Code, records that starting point. From the birthday we 'travel' nine years and our Pin Code is once more the same as it was at birth. It continues for the next nine years and the nine after that, until in all, it registers nine lives.

For the Pin Code, we 'see' the big bang as the conscious expression of our potential, and the 'black hole' aspect of our life's rotation as our 'shadow' aspect. The 'shadow' is what Carl G Jung defined as the aspects of our Persona that are refused and unacceptable to us until now. The 'shadow' is often sought by people to uncover the hidden aspects of them. Using the Human Pin Code you can see this aspect easily in the unexpressed aspects of the numbers in a person's Pin Code.

I tell the students who attend Human Pin Code workshops that we have nine 'lives' and, immediately, I get the story of a cat having nine lives. What I'm actually talking about is that after every nine years we reach a milestone; we have completed a cycle, a life stage, or a 'life'. That milestone is like a point for 'reincarnation' – the next life stage is about to start. The first eight life-stages are each nine years in duration. When we reach the ninth and final stage at age 72 (I call it the wisdom cycle) we stay in that period until we choose to die. All the other eight stages last nine years and these years each have a lesson for us to learn and experience. I will cover this in detail in Chapter 4. When you reach the next life, you can look back and say, "in my last life I learned..."

Birth is the product of a chemical reaction of the fertilization of the egg by the sperm, followed by nine months gestation period, resulting in the production of a baby. The birth of a Human Being is the start of a new micro-universe. We are identical, in atomic composition, to the Universe, our macrocosm. Our atoms rotate in the identical manner as the atoms of plants or shells, just as our solar system of planets rotate around the Sun. Our universe, the body, completes its cycle in nine-year periods. Atoms do it within seconds from our perspective, some plants within seasons and our universe within billions of years to complete its cycle.

I have enough evidence to support the theory that our mother programmed the day on which we were born. She decides (whether consciously or unconsciously) when the starting point of the new mini-universe, her new baby, will begin. For expectant mothers reading this, you are probably already aware that your mental, emotional, spiritual and physical state influences the health and development of your unborn child. When we appreciate that, and we know that the birth date imprints the personality on the child, it's not hard to surmise that a mother would influence the personality of her child.

I would like to thank Cornelia for permission to use this story about her son. She was 54 years old when she came to me for an analysis. After doing her son's Pin Code I explained to her that she had 'programmed' him during her pregnancy with him, and so 'programmed' his birth date. I added that she actually wanted a girl and not a boy. Cornelia's response was quite startling. She burst out laughing. I asked her what was so funny, so she told me this story.

When her son was born, the doctor presented her 'son' to her. She told the doctor he had made a mistake, she was expecting a girl. She even argued with the doctor that he was trying to trick her into having this 'boy!' Cornelia had prepared for her daughter's arrival by buying only pink clothes and nursery furniture. Her son had to wear the pink booties and dresses and live in his pink room until he was four.

When Cornelia's son was 17, finishing his Matric exams, he was deciding what to do as a career. His maths and physics were good and he was thinking about computer science studies. Cornelia suggested they visit her old place of employment where she worked when she was pregnant with him, since Cornelia had worked there as a computer programmer. The company for which she worked and the department were still in the same place. Cornelia had kept in contact with her ex-colleagues who were still working at the company although she hadn't been back to the building since she'd left, a week prior to her son's birth.

When Cornelia and her son arrived at the office she was completely unnerved when he stopped her at the foyer door and said, "Your desk was over there, wasn't it?" He pointed to a desk in the far corner. Cornelia was stunned. How did he know that? He then went on to identify which of the employees were her mother's ex-colleagues and where they sat when Cornelia worked there and described the employees, some who were no longer working at the company, and located where they sat. Cornelia couldn't believe he knew this information. It was evident that from within the womb he had witnessed all this. His talent and interest in computing had begun from before he was even born.

I have many case studies similar to this one.

Understanding that the Human Pin Code is a mathematical set of calculations, based on science, is important so you appreciate that an analysis is not an esoteric process. I do not rely on 'intuition' to come up with an analysis. I assess where the Pin Code is in its current rotation. By knowing this precise point, I can work backwards to see where the Pin Code has come from and determine points in time where certain events would have occurred. I can also work forward and see when future dates will put pressure on the Pin Code. This has nothing to do with 'fortune telling' or 'mystic vision'. The purpose for doing an analysis is to provide awareness to the client so they can make informed choices. Being forewarned is being forearmed. In fact, if anything, it will uncover the mystery of the mystique, thus revealing the truth.

We are only now beginning to understand that humans interpret communication very differently. A child who might be considered 'autistic' actually doesn't read body language. They hear words only. To others, words are confusing and can only be understood literally.

Verbally we use metaphors, analogies and even lie to others to convey our messages. "I had a wonderful day", can be 'translated' into, "I had a peach of a day".

The Human Pin Code is the 'alphabet' of numbers and by using the alphabet we can make up the language: the language of the Human Essence. The Human Pin Code is a numerical equation, expressed in emotional response, translated into language.

The use of this unique language of numbers allows us to deeply understand each other. This understanding leads to respect, respect leads to tolerance and tolerance leads to love.

As I've already mentioned, any professional practitioner needs to be full trained and well versed in the techniques of the Human Pin Code because they do not rely on coming up with a 'message from the other side' to give them a clue.

My definition of psychic is a person who is able to read subtle nuances that the senses cannot detect and interpret the meaning. A clairvoyant is a person who is able to read the subtle nuances that the sense cannot detect, and factor in a series of probabilities to predict an outcome.

Often people who are thought of as psychic are merely reading subtle non-verbal signals from others.

With the Human Pin Code you don't need to do that to achieve an accurate analysis. Certified practitioners are able to do an accurate analysis without seeing the person. The accuracy is so uncanny; you would think you are psychic. Readers will also be able to do analyses by studying the techniques and following the processes laid out in this book. To begin with, you might not be able to do very comprehensive readings, but practise makes perfect. The more analyses you do the better you will become. So without further ado it's time to learn how to calculate the Human Pin Code.

FIRST PRINCIPLES

The first book written on the Human Pin Code (Human Pin Code: The Sacred Maths in your Birthdate) covers the first principles of calculating and interpreting the Pin Code in detail. This chapter is a précis of the first principles in the first book and will allow any reader new to the Human Pin Code to accurately calculate the numbers and determine the elements of any Pin Code. Included in the addendum at the back of the book are the detailed descriptions of the numbers. I recommend to readers who wish to learn and understand all the details of the Human Pin Code to study the first principles in the first book.

The following chapter, Level 2 Principles, gives additional techniques to analyse the Pin Code and only after that chapter will we work on the methodology for interpretation.

CALCULATING THE HUMAN PIN CODE

The starting point to any Pin Code analysis is calculating the 8 numbers from the date of birth which make up the Human Pin Code. The basis of the calculation, the Fadic system, reduces any complex number down to a single digit, so 14 becomes $1 + 4 = 5$, 1990 becomes $1 + 9 + 9 + 0 = 19$ and then $1 + 9 = 10$ and $1 + 0 = 1$, so $1990 = 1$. A short cut is to know that any nine in a complex number is actually equivalent to zero. Check this out by reducing any complex number with a nine in it to its single digit, then replace the nine with a zero and reduce the complex number again and you'll see that this is true.

The following template is used for a Pin Code analysis. It is comprised of eight spaces in which to write the calculated numbers and when complete, is the Pin Code for the birth date.

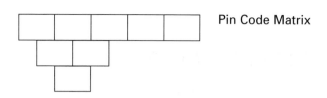

Pin Code Matrix

Using the birth date **12ᵗʰ May 1964** we start with calculating the first number in the top left hand position. It is the **day of birth,** so in this case it is a 12. We must remember to reduce numbers to a single digit so 1 + 2 = 3. Write the three in the top left hand position. This position is called the **personality.**

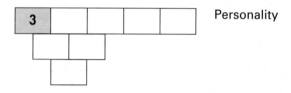

Personality

The second position on the top line, or **social consciousness,** is the **month of birth**. For our example of 12ᵗʰ May 1964 or 12/5/1964, the month May is a 5. A December birthday (12ᵗʰ month) would reduce down to a 3 (1 + 2 = 3). Write the five in the second box to represent the social consciousness.

Social consciousness

The third position on the top line is the **year of birth**. Our example year is 1964. You add the numbers together 1 + 9 + 6 + 4 = 20, reduce the 20 by adding 2 + 0 = 2 (or as mentioned you exclude the nine because you know it is equivalent to a zero and add 1 + 6 + 4 = 11, reduce this number by adding 1 + 1 = 2). This position is called the **global consciousness**.

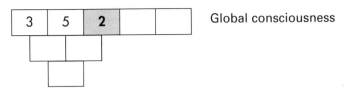

Global consciousness

The next number on the top line is calculated by **adding the numbers in the first three positions**. Add all three numbers that are in the template 3 + 5 + 2 = 10, and then reduce this number down to its single digit, 1 + 0 = 1. The number in the fourth position on the top line is called the **life cycle** number.

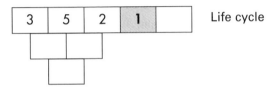

Life cycle

The final figure in the top row of numbers is the **lesson** number. You determine it by **adding the life cycle with the personality** number. In this example 3 + 1 = 4.

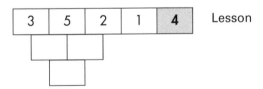

Lesson

The left hand position in the second row is calculated by adding the two numbers above it, the **personality plus the social consciousness**. The number in this position is the **inner self** and in this example is 8 (3 from the personality plus 5 from the social consciousness equals 8).

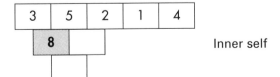

Inner self

The right hand position in the second row is the **inner child** and is calculated in a similar way – add the two numbers above, the **social consciousness plus the global consciousness**. Add 5 + 2 = 7.

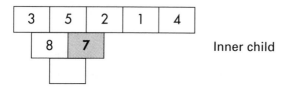

Inner child

The final position on the Pin Code is at the bottom and is called the **sense of spirit**. It is calculated by adding the two numbers from the row above. **Add inner self to the inner child**, 8 + 7 = 15 and then reduce 15, 1 + 5 = 6. The sense of spirit in this example is 6.

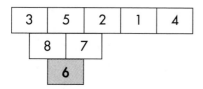

Sense of spirit

The Pin Code is complete when all 8 positions have been calculated.

To practise the calculation of the Pin Code use your birth date and complete the following template:

Birth date:_____

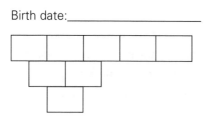

The essence of each number is described later in this chapter and the full description of the numbers is found in the addendum.

POSITIONS IN THE PIN CODE TEMPLATE

The Pin Code Matrix has eight positions each referring to an aspect of our overall personality.

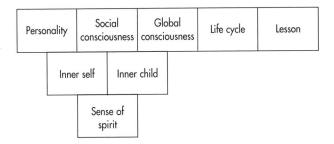

Personality

The number in the **personality** position comes from a person's birth day – a Three in our example – can also be called the Public Persona. It represents a person's perception of his *external* reality and the manner in which he or she interacts with that reality. It is a person's perception of him or herself, their capacity to think and ability to feel and act. It is the personality that is projected to the outside world most of the time, and it sets the general tone of the external personality. When thinking about another person and we say, "What a nice person" or "She's rather quiet" it is the **personality** that we perceive.

The personality is the first and primary number I always look at in a individual Pin Code. It has the strongest influence on a person's behaviour. When you learn the essence of the each number (from One to Nine) you will be able to get a quick assessment on someone just by knowing their day of birth. Clearly it's by no means the only influence on their behaviour, otherwise we would not need all the other numbers. It is, however, a strong influence.

Social consciousness

When at home, most of us act differently from when we are out. When we deal with intimate relationships, we are functioning primarily through our personality number. The aspects of our character with which we function when we step out of the front door and into society, is our **social consciousness**. This number is how we deal with people on a more superficial level, or those whom we don't know so well – such as acquaintances and colleagues in the workplace.

As a quick reference, if you are doing an analysis for someone you don't know well, check out their social consciousness to see how they will respond to your analysis. A Seven in this position will feel uncomfortable with you delving into their "secrets" because Sevens are private people. A Five, as is our example, will talk over you and want to answer back to everything. Learning the essence of each number will give you a quick reference and help you with your analyses.

Global consciousness

The **global consciousness** represents the evolutionary, progressive state of the world in a given year. Each year contains the influences of the prevalent ideas in politics, technology, art and literature. These are picked up via the media, such as by listening to the news, where there is no *direct* contact with the people involved. The mother perceives these influences during her pregnancy, and imprints them onto her child.

There are millions of people born every year who will have the same number in the global consciousness position. The birth date we are using in our example, 12th May 1964 has a global consciousness of Two. People born in 1973 and 1982 also have the same global consciousness as those born in 1964. However you must take into account that there is a different decade influence prevailing on the global influence. Those born in the 1970s in the 'flower power' era will perceive the world in a different way from those born into the technology explosion of the 1990s.

The global consciousness indicates your view of the world. Someone with an Eight in their global consciousness will think the world is driven by business and big corporations whilst a person with a Five in this position will see the world as a place for adventure and exploration. The influence of the decade will determine how adventure is expressed. In the 1970s exploration was done in the mind with the use of drugs, whilst the 1990s see exploration using technology. Perhaps a Five global consciousness in the 2010s decade will experience space exploration?

Life cycle

The **life cycle** number predicts what the person should strive towards, in order to maintain balance and harmony within the Pin Code, during periods of upheaval and change. It's your 'tool box', a resource you can draw on when things change. Someone with a One in their life cycle will take charge, whilst a Three in the life cycle will find someone else to sort out the problem. A person with a Nine in this position will seem to manage periods of change with fewer problems than others.

Lesson

This number represents the **lesson** that the person has come to learn. The lesson is to minimise the 'reactive' aspects of the number. An open and honest look at these attributes provides valuable information for a person's personal growth.

Inner self

The **inner self** represents our subconscious personality. It determines our unconscious instincts and how we will react in situations of excitement. Faced with elation, we will generally express the active side of the number in this position, but in a crisis it is probably the reactive side that will emerge.

It is always good to look at the personality number and the inner self number and see if there is potential conflict here as this is what will play out as inner tension for the person. An example of this is a person with a Two personality. This makes them a nurturing, caring but potentially timid person. And if this person has a One in the inner self position they subconsciously feel they are a leader which could potentially be in conflict with how they are perceived.

Inner child / Comfort zone

The **inner child** or, as I now refer to it, the **comfort zone** shows how we will react when put on a stage or are in the public arena. This is evident in children when they are growing up. As we begin growing into adulthood from about the age of sixteen or seventeen, there is a transition from the childlike inner child, towards the inner self.

This does not mean, however, that in adulthood we will never display the inner child. Most people will still experience situations when the inner child emerges such, as when we're put on the spot, out of our comfort zone. Some of the best actors (such as Brad Pitt) have a Four in this position because the Four is able to perform in such situations.

The inner child number can be very reactive if that person was emotionally wounded in their formative years. If the wounding was particularly traumatic, or the person achieves great power and wealth in their later years, the inner child can sometimes 'take over' the inner self. A spoilt brat syndrome can prevail in a 60 year-old man.

Sense of spirit

The **sense of spirit** literally represents the 'spirit' in which we do things. A person with a Six in this position will always enjoy creating harmonious and happy social gatherings while a person with an Eight in this position will operate from a place of what they can get out of the situation. This is a key position in the Synergy Pin Code for two people as it will determine the spirit of the relationship.

THE ELEMENTS

A very important aspect of the Human Pin Code and also easily interpreted, is the 'element' that is associated with each number. I use 'elements' rather than academic terms because it's simple and easy to remember; air, water, fire and earth. Air corresponds with the intellect (head in the clouds type stuff), water is emotion, fire is drive or spiritedness and earth is practicality (salt of the earth).

Eight of the numbers are associated with an element as follows:
The **air** numbers are **One** and **Five**
The **water** numbers are **Two** and **Seven**
The **fire** numbers are **Three** and **Six**
The **earth** numbers are **Four** and **Eight**

For those more academically inclined the intellectual processing numbers are One and Five. The emotional processing numbers are Two and Seven. The spirited (or driven) numbers are Three and Six. The practical numbers are Four and Eight.

The number that is missing is the **Nine**. I mentioned earlier that when you add a nine to any number it behaves as if it's zero (remember adding 1+9=1, 5+9=5, etc.), so the nine has a unique place with no element associated with it.

The elements help describe a person. The number of elements present and the quantity of each element in a Pin Code are quickly identifiable. Take the example we used in learning to calculate the Pin Code, 12th May 1964: we use the Pin Code to determine the number of elements in it and write it in a table. The Pin Code is:

3	5	2	1	4

8	7

6

	Elements
Air	
Water	
Fire	
Earth	
Nine	N/A

Element table

In our example count the number of air elements. Air elements are represented by the numbers One and Five. There is a One and a Five in the Pin Code, so two air elements in total. Write '2' in the table in the row titled "Air". Now count the number of water elements. Water is represented by Twos and Sevens. There is a Two and a Seven in the Pin Code making a total of two water elements. Write '2' in the row titled 'Water'. Fire is represented by numbers Three and Six. This Pin Code has one Three and one Six, so the count for fire elements is two and should be written in the row for Fire. There are two earth numbers in the Pin Code represented by one Four and one Eight so there is a total of two earth elements. Write '2' in the earth row. There are no Nines in the Pin Code, but if there were, they wouldn't be counted in the elements table because Nine doesn't have an associated element.

	Elements
Air	2
Water	2
Fire	2
Earth	2
Nine	N/A

Air numbers are **One** and **Five**

Water numbers are **Two** and **Seven**

Fire numbers are **Three** and **Six**

Earth numbers are **Four** and **Eight**

Practise calculating the elements in your own Pin Code which you calculated earlier in the chapter and add up the number of air elements (Ones and Fives). Count the water elements (Twos and Sevens). Count the fire elements (Threes and Sixes) and finally count the earth elements (Fours and Eights). Use the following table to record the elements in your Pin Code.

	Elements
Air	
Water	
Fire	
Earth	
Nine	N/A

The elements are used early in a Pin Code analysis as it gives the practitioner a quick handle on the type of person being analysed. If, as in the example we used 12th May 1964, there are two of each element, we would determine this person to be well balanced. In another Pin Code there could be five water elements and you would know this person is overly emotional. When there is a Pin Code with lots of fire this person will be very energetic with lots of drive and potentially could be explosive.

One of the reasons to use the terminology of the elements rather than the academic names, is because it is easy to remember and easy to interpret. If a Pin Code has a high count for the earth and fire elements you can surmise that there is a lot of smouldering going on in this person (earth can put out fire or keep it under control). With a lot of air and water in a Pin Code the person will be very bubbly (air bubbles through water). A Pin Code with a lot of earth will indicate a very grounded solid person, and if most of the numbers were earth they maybe too strongly grounded and be overly stubborn.

The elements become very important in the Synergy analysis which we will do later in the book.

THE ESSENCE OF THE NUMBERS

Giving each number an essence description provides a starting point when elaborating on the many attributes of each number. The descriptions of the numbers are interpreted in the different positions. For example, if we describe a One in the personality as being "a strong leader, with a sweeping creative energy", then a One in the inner child position would mean that he aspires to display those qualities, while in inner self position it would mean that he only shows these attributes to those close to him, or when he is under pressure.

Each number has an active and reactive side to it. Ideally, when a person is in balance, the active and reactive side will balance but often in times of stress, or if a person has experienced trauma in some period of their life, the reactive side will be dominant. The challenge for each of us is to recognise when we are operating in the reactive side of the number and work at minimising it and replacing it with a more active aspect.

The detail of each number is referenced in the addendum, we are including here just a brief overview of each number. Readers who are serious about learning to analyse Pin Codes are strongly recommended to thoroughly learn the detail of the numbers.

One – The Creator
The first number, the creator, the leader. Image conscious and talkative, the One likes everyone to do it their way. One is associated with the element 'air'.

Two – The Nurturer
Number Two is the mothering energy, nurturing, caring and deeply emotional. Quiet, homely and domesticated the Two is associated with the element 'water'.

Three – The Organiser
Organised, independent and optimistic, the number Three is serious and ambitious and can be deeply religious. With plenty of drive, the

Three is associated with the element 'fire'.

Four – The Investigator
The Four number is eccentric and offbeat, perceptive and purposeful and can be a bit cynical. Four is associated with the element 'earth'.

Five – The Analyst
Humorous and extrovert, the Five is intellectual and rebellious. When in its reactive aspect it can be stressed and volatile. Five is associated with the element 'air'.

Six – The Charmer
Charming, romantic, sensual and affectionate is the number Six. If unbalanced it can become self absorbed and demanding. The Six is associated with the element 'fire'.

Seven – The Dignified
Quiet and conservative, the Seven can also take it to extreme and seem aloof. The Seven is associated with the element of 'water'.

Eight – The Dependable
Eight is the number of stability, responsibility and is worldly-wise. When out of balance the Eight can be insecure and manipulative and feels victimised. The Eight is associated with the element of 'earth'.

Nine – The Child
The Nine is unique, idealist and naïve which can turn to be forgetful, impulsive and vain. The Nine has no element associated with it.

These are the first principles of the Human Pin Code. You are now able to calculate the Pin Code from any birth date. You can determine the number of each element in a Pin Code. You will know each position in the Pin Code and also know the essence of each number.

We haven't yet covered the methodology for interpreting the Pin Code because now I want to share with you new information which further refines the analysis of the Human Pin Code.

LEVEL TWO PRINCIPLES

It is important that the reader is well versed in the first principles of the Human Pin Code. These principles are covered in detail in the first book written on the subject Human Pin Code: The Sacred Maths in your Birthdate. They are in abbreviated form in the previous chapter. The new techniques I am about to share with you require your knowledge in the first principles.

In this chapter you will learn how to calculate the life stage matrix of the Pin Code. This matrix will allow you to quickly identify how the person is influenced by the different energies of the year.

I have also developed a simple calculation which determines a person's processing style. I'm sure you've heard the saying "she wears the pants" or "he's in touch with his feminine side". These are the type of comments referring to the way in which the person operates. It is particularly useful to compare a processing style with the gender of the person. Often at birth our parents put us in the 'pink box' for girls or 'blue box' for boys and we are expected to behave in the traditional way suitable for a boy or a girl. I'm generalising but you'll get the point – girls in touch with their feminine side and boys strong and macho who don't cry.

As time has moved on we are finding more women operating in traditionally masculine environments (there are more women taking first year engineering courses at University than ever before) and men who are comfortable in expressing their feminine or passive style. I want to make it clear up front that the processing style does not determine sexual orientation. A passive processing style does not indicate that a man is gay and a dominant processing style does not indicate that a woman is lesbian.

These processing styles have had us confused. Now the Human Pin Code reveals the true processing style.

After learning how to calculate the processing style, we will combine all the techniques and calculations we have learnt in this, and the previous chapter, into an interpretation of a Pin Code.

CALCULATING THE LIFE STAGE

As I have already mentioned, there are nine life stages each lasting nine years. The first four stages are the learning phases for a human, the time of knowledge and the next five stages are the time for experience.

The life stages we go through are:

Nursery	0 – 9 years	
Teenage	9 – 18 years	
Bachelor	18 – 27 years	Learning stages
Nesting	27 – 36 years	
Adulthood	36 – 45 years	
Spiritual	45 – 54 years	
Family	54 – 63 years	Experience stages
Achievement	63 – 72 years	
Wisdom	72 onwards	

The first life stage starts at birth and is called the **nursery stage**. As with the numbers in the Pin Code, these stages also have elements associated with them. The nursery stage is the first stage, being associated with air is related to learning and developing the intellect. Additionally you can look back and see that at age 4 when a child learns the difference between truth and lies, this child learnt it in the manner of the life cycle number. If the child's life cycle number in that year is an Eight, we know that Eight gives ambitious and protective energy. A child aged four operating with an Eight in his life cycle may well learn how to lie when protecting his toys from other children. "No, I don't have a Barbie doll," he says sitting on the toy box hiding the doll in question.

A child at four with a life cycle of Four will learn the lesson of truth versus lies in a very straight forward way. If the life cycle is a Seven the child will learn secretively. It's important to learn the nuances of the effect of the life cycle number on the life stage.

The second stage, the **teenage stage**, starts at nine years old and is associated with the number Two, the development of emotions. Children at this time learn how far to push their boundaries and experience the highs and lows of their emotions. I find there is enormous pressure on children of this age to meet the expectations of their parents: to be the success their parents want them to be, particularly if the parents have a traditional view of their children (the 'pink' or 'blue' box concept). For passive processing boys this can be too much pressure as they are unable to be the dominant boy their father or mother wants them to be. As for dominant girls, they rebel against their parent's desires for them to be soft and feminine. The expectations of our religion and culture can also pressurise the teenager into behaving in a certain way.

I have many clients with teenage children who are literally tearing their hair out in frustration, as their sons withdraw from family life, and their daughters rebel into a gothic phase. The children's rebellion is their way of trying to assert some form of control on their life. They feel enormous frustration when their true identity is not recognized or appreciated. It's a sad fact that teenage suicide has increased in recent years and I do believe the lack of recognition of the teenager's identity is the core of this problem.

When you do a Pin Code analysis on your teenager's birth date and objectively review your expectations and desires for your child, your spouse's expectations and your culture's expectations, you will begin to understand why their behaviour might not be as sociable as you'd like it to be.

The most important aspect to consider when having babies is to understand how they process through understanding their Pin Code. Every child needs to be stimulated constantly, using all of the senses, to develop into a well rounded person. They will be able to express the love, connection and manners that we all admire. This behaviour commands respect no matter what age you are.

If you think that corporal punishment or enthusiasm for discipline is the answer, all you are teaching the child is how to 'love' by being aggressive. Teach the child respect and love and they won't fight or be rebellious. 'Panel-beat' the child and you will teach a nation how to go to war.

The third stage is the **bachelor stage** (or for those who want it to be politically correct the bachelor / bachelorette stage. However, it is a bold, dominant energy associated with this stage so the 'bachelor' title is appropriate). It starts at 18 and finishes at 27 years and is associated with the element of fire. It is the life stage where drive and passion are embraced.

The child in the nursery stage will learn about love through absorption but teaching the child in their teenage years about love is more prescriptive. They need to know how to go about this task. Many grown adults haven't had this training and as they progress through their life, fall foul of love. Without this training we arrive in our Bachelor years which are influenced by the fire element (passion, drive, spiritedness) with no idea how to manage these heady days of romance. In these years we fall in love with love and then look for someone to do it with, so whoever comes along we will fall in love with them! A person in a Six life cycle year in the bachelor stage will not only be in love with love, but also will want children.

I see many young clients in their bachelor phase and some of the women are obsessed with finding a husband and having children. I strongly counsel them to wait. Live together, have fun. In the bachelor stage it's hard to see beyond passion and lust, and often it's mistaken for love. By appreciating that it's love you're in love with, not the person, you will be able to enjoy the time without the expectations of 'happily ever after'. Not until we are in our adulthood stage (after 36) will we really understand what true love is and what is right for us.

A person this age should be encouraged to channel their drive and passion into other avenues rather than early nesting. I have found that the more breadth of learning in the bachelor stage, the greater the building in the nesting stage – more money, more success, and more fulfillment.

The **nesting stage**, from 27 to 36 years, culminates in rewards from your previous life stages. All studies and learning you undertake in the years prior to nesting will be returned in success and money, exponentially. If you have had heavy responsibilities in your bachelor years with a spouse and children, unless you have a lot of money to provide the care needed for your family, you will have had to disempower your learning abilities in these important bachelor years. The bachelor years, with all the enthusiasm and drive, sets you up to build great empires in your nesting stage.

We need to remember that when life expectancy was only 40 – 45 years it was important to reproduce early to keep the population going. Now we have a life expectancy into our late 60s or 70s, we have more years in which to bring up our children and preserve our population. The primal urge to mate in our early years will still raise its head so to speak but err on the side of caution here if you possibly can, unless you can afford to study and learn and bring up a family all at the same time.

These first four stages, nursery, teenage, bachelor and nesting, are knowledge stages where we learn as much as we can. The next four stages are experience stages where we modify our knowledge with the experiences. I'm sure younger readers will have had older people say, "Youth is wasted on the young!" Exasperating as it is when you hear it, what they are trying to tell you is that all the knowledge in the world can't take the place of life's experiences.

After all the hard work of the bachelor and nesting stages, when you get to the **adulthood stage** (36 to 45 years), you'll be wanting to enjoy what you've built. You won't want to work so hard and your passion for the job, or project, will drive you rather than survival needs. Because survival isn't the priority many people fritter away the hard earned cash of the previous years. Also, in the adult stage, as it's an air stage, a thinking stage, we re-evaluate our lives. This is the first stage in our experience phase (from adulthood to wisdom) and we are able to look back at our four stages of learning and decide what we like best, what we missed out on and what we'd like to do now. I always advise people in their Four life cycle year in this stage to be extra aware that change is afoot. You can embrace change or you can resist it. Either way you will experience change during this time.

The next stage is the **spiritual stage** (45 to 54 years) when we ask "Who am I?" We have to learn about ourselves in this stage. I encourage everyone to do so but without giving away their power. Too many seekers have found their guru, given their money away and professed to have found their nirvana. Do yourself a favour – open a trust account and put all your money in it before you go on your pilgrimage. There is nothing worse than leaving your mountain top having found your Self to find yourself broke at 53!

The **family stage** (54 to 63 years) gives us the desire to retire at 55, down scale the responsibilities and socialise. It's about enjoyment and if you've achieved your lessons in the previous life stages you'll have enough money and security to do just that. However, if you have given all your money to the Guru, or lost it in an amazing new get rich quick venture during your adult years, you'll be relying on your children to get you through these years.

The eighth phase is that of the **achievement stage** from 63 to 71 years. You don't need to achieve, you need to acknowledge your achievements. Many successful business people are asked to go onto company boards to be non-executive directors at this time. If the previous lessons are still wanting and you're financially dependent on your children they will try to get you into a home as quickly as they can!

At 72 years, with a sigh of relief we move into our **wisdom stage** and sit back. From our experience will be able to tell everyone else how to live their life!

When we miss one of these stages or experience the stages 'out of sequence', I find that a person's life is beset with difficulties. It's not to say that this is prescriptive and you must follow the stages as specified. I am suggesting that when the effort is made to develop the skills needed in each stage at the right time, it will be rewarded later in life.

Carmen is a very good example of this. She married in her bachelor years to a man a few years older than her so he was in his nesting stage ready to be married. As a couple they were well liked. They had good careers and travelled overseas regularly. Carmen's career began to really take off as she hit her nesting years (at 27). She found it hard to put her finger on exactly what triggered the problems in her marriage, but she did say, "I suddenly woke up one morning, looked at the man sleeping next to me and knew I couldn't have children with him. It just wasn't right."

Carmen, by this time, was deep in her nesting phase, the earth element was evident in her career building and now she wanted to build a family and this wasn't the man with whom she wanted to do it. She acknowledged to me that when she met her husband she didn't know what 'love' really was and now, with many years hindsight she appreciated that the 'love' she felt for this man way back then, as a young woman in her twenties wasn't 'love' as she knows it now. It wasn't that she didn't want children (and in fact now has children with her new husband) and it wasn't her career that was over-riding her decision. It was her choice of first husband – he just wasn't the right man for her, but at 23 she couldn't see that. She acknowledges now that she was being driven by family pressures, societal pressures and her lust to be married.

Another client, Daniel was 39 and in his adulthood phase, when he started visiting a local bar on his way home from work. Initially his work mate had invited him for a quick drink but he found the other clientele equally as interesting and continued to frequent the place. They were young, pretty, nubile and great fun. His quick drink became a couple of glasses which became a bottle or two shared with some of the very pretty girls. His wife of 18 years and their three teenage sons waited at home.

Daniel's slide down the slippery slope into infidelity was pretty quick. Within a year he was separated from his wife and living with a 23 year-old woman. No one could understand why he had done it, least of all his wife. Everyone decided he was having a mid-life crisis.

Daniel had hit his adulthood stage and had questioned his life. What was he doing? Eighteen years married, three teenage boys, successful business. No fun. His early marriage at 21 years of age had given him nesting responsibilities well before he was ready for them. His adulthood life stage made him think about all the things he'd missed out on.

It's not to say that if you missed a certain phase it gives you permission to go back and find it, destroying what you have and anything else that gets in your way. The purpose of sharing Daniel's story is to show how the subconscious works. Had Daniel been warned that these thoughts and energies would prevail in his adulthood stage he may have found an alternative way of reassessing his life. It could have fulfilled his need for change and caused less destruction to everyone around him.

I warn people in this stage that the money they accumulated in the nesting phase is often lost in these years. It seems to be frittered away and by the end of the nine year stage, you awake broke, wondering what on earth you have to do now to survive through retirement.

To calculate the life stage, you need to think about it as a nine by nine matrix. This matrix is very valuable for any Pin Code analysis as it enables you to pin-point specific periods in this person's life. Use the matrix template from the back of the book or draw one up with nine years along the top, starting from birth (year 0) until nine. On the other axis write the life stage starting with the nursery stage, then the teenage stage, bachelor stage and so on.

Life cycle: Nursery Year:									
	0	1	2	3	4	5	6	7	8
Teenage	9	10	11	12	13	14	15	16	17
Bachelor	18	19	20	21	22	23	and so on...		

To populate the life stage matrix we will use the birth date from the previous chapter – 12th May 1964. We know the birth date 12th May 1964 has the Pin Code:

Life Cycle number

We also know the life cycle number is in the fourth position in the top row of the Pin Code. You will recall it's calculated by adding the first three positions in the top row; in this case we add 3 + 5 + 2 = 10 then reduce the 10 down to a single digit, so 1 + 0 = 1. The life cycle number for this birth date is One.

When this person was born in 1964 their life cycle number at point zero (birth) was One. We write in the life cycle number in our matrix on the top line. As each year progresses so does the life cycle number, so in when the child is one, the life cycle number is 1 + 1 = 2; when they are two, the life cycle number progresses another year to Three and so on. When the life cycle number plus year reaches 10 (one plus nine years), we do what we always do with complex numbers and reduce it to a single digit; 10 reduces to 1 + 0 = 1.

We write in the year of birth on the line below the zero and we continue the years sequentially.

Life cycle:	1	2	3	4	5	6	7	8	9
Nursery	0	1	2	3	4	5	6	7	8
Year:	1964	1965	1966	1967	1968	1969	1970	1971	1972
	1	2	3	4	5	6	7	8	9
Teenage	9	10	11	12	13	14	15	16	17
	1973	1974	1975	1976	1977	1978	1979	1980	1981
	1	2	3	4	5	6	7	8	9
Bachelor	18	19	20	21	22	23	24	25	26
	1982	1983	1984	1985	1986	1987	1988	1989	1990
	1	2	3	4	5	6	7	8	9
Nesting	27	28	29	30	31	32	33	34	35
	1991	1992	1993	1994	1995	1996	1997	1998	1999
	1	2	3	4	5	6	7	8	9
Adulthood	36	37	38	39	40	41	42	43	44
	2000	2001	2002	2003	2004	2005	2006	2007	2008

Spiritual	45	46	47	48	49	50	51	52	53
Family	54	55	56	57	58	59	60	61	62
Achievement	63	64	65	66	67	68	69	70	71
Wisdom	72	And onwards							

You will notice that the life cycle number starts at the same number (in this case One) at the beginning of each life stage. This is the beginning of our next new life stage, our next nine year rotation. It's an important milestone. With the use of the Human Pin Code we can predict what lessons we will be learning and when we'll be learning them.

The value of doing this matrix is that you can immediately see how this person will be operating in any given year. Take the year 2004. This person is forty, in their adulthood stage, operating as a Five in their life cycle. You can then determine that for their adult development they will be looking for inventive and adventurous ways to explore this. The previous year (2003) was a Four year for this person and Four years challenge our perception. In the adulthood stage, a Four year will make us think of what we missed out on and what we really want to do.

The One year in 2000 would have been about new beginnings. Whatever was started in this year will culminate in 2008 (an Eight year is about completion). The Nine year in 2009 will be about new ideas and preparing for the new One year about to start in 2010.

Take time now to develop your own life cycle matrix. Firstly, write in your year of birth in the first column directly below the zero and continue the years until your current age (or more if you wish). Now go to your Pin Code and write your life cycle number to the first column above the zero. Remember your life cycle number is the number in the fourth position on the top row of your Pin Code.

Life cycle: Nursery Year:	0	1	2	3	4	5	6	7	8
Teenage	9	10	11	12	13	14	15	16	17
Bachelor	18	19	20	21	22	23	24	25	26
Nesting	27	28	29	30	31	32	33	34	35
Adulthood	36	37	38	39	40	41	42	43	44
Spiritual	45	46	47	48	49	50	51	52	53
Family	54	55	56	57	58	59	60	61	62
Achievement	63	64	65	66	67	68	69	70	71
Wisdom	72	And onwards							

We know that One years are new beginnings and Four years can be upheaval and change. Look at your life cycle matrix and identify key times in your life and determine whether there is a pattern.

Carmen, the woman who had married early in her bachelor years had such a shock when I did this matrix with her. She discovered that she was in a Six year (passion, family, lust and sex) when she married her first husband. She was also in a Six year when she became engaged to her second husband! She was in a Four year when she separated from her first husband. I've warned her to be careful when the next Four year approaches to be sure she channels the energies of change in her relationship with her second husband in a positive way – well that's if she wants to stay married to him!

Use your life stage matrix to predict what you might encounter in your love life, your career and with your family in the next year.

PROCESSING STYLE

Now we will learn about the Pin Code's processing style. Each number has a processing energy. In the first book written on the Human Pin Code, I referred to the processing style as 'flexible' and 'inflexible'. These terms don't do the numbers sufficient justice and I have now called them 'dominant' and 'passive' processing styles. You could define dominant processing as more masculine energy and passive as feminine energy, but these terms are limiting and you might become fixated on gender issues. Think of dominant processing style as active, action oriented energy and passive processing as creative, gentler energy.

You will recall the elements table in the previous chapter where you filled in the number of elements in your Pin Code. We extend this table to add the processing style by adding two new columns.

	Elements	Dominant	Passive
Air			
Water			
Fire			
Earth			
Nine	N/A		

The dominant energy numbers are:	The passive energy numbers are:
One	Five
Three	Two
Six	Four
Eight	Seven

Still using our birth date example of 12th May 1964 we recall the Pin Code and element count:

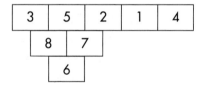

3	5	2	1	4
	8	7		
		6		

	Elements	Dominant	Passive
Air	2		
Water	2		
Fire	2		
Earth	2		
Nine	N/A		

When you are familiar with the processing style for each number and have practised this a few times you may be able to do the processing calculation by simply counting up the numbers in the Pin Code. However, until you are confident in doing this, I recommend you use the table.

To calculate the processing style for this Pin Code we first count the dominant numbers. We know that numbers One, Three, Six and Eight are all dominant numbers. There is one One in the Pin Code so we write One in the air row in the dominant column.

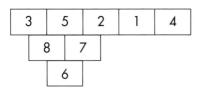

	Elements	Dominant	Passive
Air	2	**1**	
Water	2	N/A	
Fire	2		
Earth	2		
Nine	N/A		

Both water numbers, Two and Seven, are passive so the dominant position in the water row in the table is never filled.

The next dominant numbers to count are the fire numbers. Both fire numbers, Three and Six, are dominant so we count the total number of Threes and Sixes in the Pin Code. There is one Three and one Six so we write the count of two in the fire row in the dominant column. As in this Pin Code both fire numbers are dominant so we never write in anything in the passive column in the fire row.

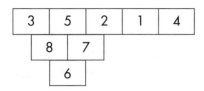

	Elements	Dominant	Passive
Air	2	1	
Water	2	N/A	
Fire	2	**2**	N/A
Earth	2		
Nine	N/A		

Now we count the dominant earth numbers which is the Eight. There is one Eight in this Pin Code, which we now write in the earth row in the dominant column.

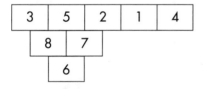

	Elements	Dominant	Passive
Air	2	1	
Water	2	N/A	
Fire	2	2	N/A
Earth	2	**1**	
Nine	N/A		

Next we count the passive numbers in the Pin Code. Numbers Two, Four, Five and Seven are all passive.

There is one passive air number (Five), which is in the global consciousness position. We write the count of one in the air row in the passive column.

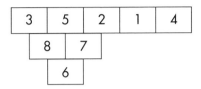

	Elements	Dominant	Passive
Air	2	1	**1**
Water	2	N/A	
Fire	2	2	N/A
Earth	2	1	
Nine	N/A		

We know that both water numbers (Two and Seven) are passive numbers and this Pin Code has one of each so the count of two is written in the water row in the passive column.

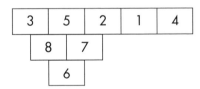

	Elements	Dominant	Passive
Air	2	1	1
Water	2	N/A	**2**
Fire	2	2	N/A
Earth	2	1	
Nine	N/A		

Fire is dominant only so we don't write anything in the passive column for fire, but the Four is a passive earth number and this Pin Code has one Four in the lesson position. We write the count of one in the passive column in the earth row.

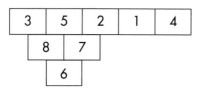

	Elements	Dominant	Passive
Air	2	1	1
Water	2	N/A	2
Fire	2	2	N/A
Earth	2	1	**1**
Nine	N/A		

It's helpful to remember that the two fire numbers (Three and Six) are both dominant numbers whilst the two water numbers (Two and Seven) are both passive. Only with the air and earth numbers do you have to be careful to be sure you put them in the correct dominant or passive position.

The Nine we know, is a special number with no element allocated to it. It does, however, have a processing energy which is different from all the other numbers. We will cover how to calculate the Nine's processing style in the next example. In the meantime this Pin Code does not contain a Nine, so we write zero in each position on the table for the Nine row.

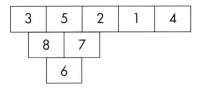

	Elements	Dominant	Passive
Air	2	1	1
Water	2	N/A	2
Fire	2	2	N/A
Earth	2	1	1
Nine	N/A	**0**	**0**
Total	N/A		

This element / processing style table is now almost complete. The last task to undertake is to add up the numbers in the dominant and passive columns

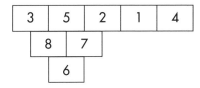

	Elements	Dominant	Passive
Air	2	1	1
Water	2	N/A	2
Fire	2	2	N/A
Earth	2	1	1
Nine	N/A	0	0
Total	N/A	**4**	**4**

4/4 dominant / passive processing

As a double check, add the numbers in the rows across – there is one dominant and one passive number in the air row (1 + 1 = 2) and there are two air elements so this is correct: 1 dominant air + 1 passive air = 2 air elements.

Two water elements will both be in the passive column. Two fire elements will both be in the dominant column.

There is one dominant earth and one passive earth which make two earth elements. This is also correct in the table.

We haven't yet dealt with the number Nine. We know from the previous chapter that it doesn't have an element associated with it, and when determining the processing style it is also treated differently to the other numbers. We know that Nine is equivalent to zero and if you add 1 + 2 + 3 + 4 + 5 + 6 + 7 + 8 it equals 36, reduce 36 to a single digit and what do you get? 3 + 6 = 9. Nine includes all the numbers. In determining the processing style we use Nine as both dominant and passive. For each Nine in a Pin Code you add 0.5 to the dominant column and 0.5 to the passive column.

As an example if you take the birthday 9th September 1989 you will get the following Pin Code:

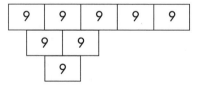

When you calculate the elements and dominant and passive processing style for this Pin Code you will know firstly that the Nine has no element associated with it and secondly for processing style every Nine in a Pin Code is counted as 0.5 for the dominant processing style and 0.5 for the passive processing style. There are eight Nines in the Pin Code so 0.5 + 0.5 + 0.5 + 0.5 + 0.5 + 0.5 + 0.5 + 0.5 = 4 dominant. The same calculation is done for the passive numbers so the answer is 4 passive.

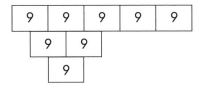

	Elements	Dominant	Passive
Air	0	0	0
Water	0	N/A	0
Fire	0	0	N/A
Earth	0	0	0
Nine	N/A	4	4
Total	N/A	4	4

4/4 dominant / passive

As this can be a little confusing let's do another birth date as an example. Take 2nd March 1981. Use the Pin Code template and table below to do your calculations then read on to find the answer.

Birth date: 2nd March 1981

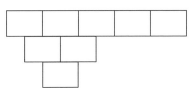

	Elements	Dominant	Passive
Air			
Water		N/A	
Fire			N/A
Earth			
Nine	N/A		
Total	N/A		

If you ended up with a total score of 4.5 in the dominant column and 3.5 in the passive column you have the correct answer. This is how you work it out:

Birth date: **2ⁿᵈ March 1981**

Firstly calculate the Pin Code. Go back to the previous chapter if you have forgotten the steps. If you calculated it correctly you will have the following numbers in the template:

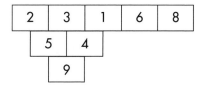

Now add up the elements. How many air (Ones and Fives)? Water (Twos and Sevens)? Fire (Threes and Sixes)? Earth (Four and Eights)? Add these to the first column in the table.

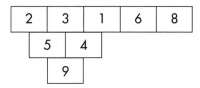

	Elements	Dominant	Passive
Air	2		
Water	1	N/A	
Fire	2		N/A
Earth	2		
Nine	N/A		
Total	N/A		

Now determine how many dominant numbers there are. We know the dominant numbers are One, Three, Six and Eight. This Pin Code has one of each of those numbers, so write the correct count in the dominant column corresponding to the correct element. Remember to count up the Three and the Six and write two in the fire row.

The passive numbers are Two, Four, Five and Seven. This Pin Code does not contain a Seven, so write the other three numbers, in the passive column, against the corresponding element.

Now we have to deal with the Nine. We know that the processing style of the Nine is determined by adding 0.5 to the dominant column and 0.5 to the passive column for every Nine in the Pin Code. There is only one Nine in this Pin Code, so we add 0.5 to the dominant column and 0.5 to the passive column.

Now we add the two columns and write the totals in the bottom row.

2	3	1	6	8

	5	4		

	9			

	Elements	Dominant	Passive
Air	2	1	1
Water	1	N/A	1
Fire	2	2	N/A
Earth	2	1	1
Nine	N/A	0.5	0.5
Total	N/A	4.5	3.5

If you do many Pin Code calculations, you will find the maximum dominant score you can achieve is 7.5, with its corresponding 0.5 passive score. The maximum passive score is also 7.5 and it has a corresponding dominant score of 0.5.

When we read the dominant / passive score we only refer to the highest figure, so in this example this Pin Code is *4.5 dominant.*

For our earlier examples of 6th February 1994 and 9th September 1980 we have a score of 4 dominant and 4 passive and in this case where the processing styles are equal we refer to it as *4/4*.

There is a continuum for the processing style, the centre being 4/4 and to left the dominant scores increase by 0.5 from 4.5, 5.0, 5.5 all the way to 7.5. On the right side the passive scores increase by 0.5 from 4.5, 5.0 and so on, to 7.5.

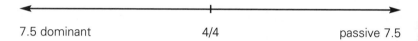

7.5 dominant   4/4   passive 7.5

A score of 7.5 dominant is more dominant than a score of 4.5 dominant. However the 4.5 dominant is still dominant. It is rather like being pregnant, you can't be half pregnant or just a little bit pregnant. You are either dominant or passive, or 4/4. The stronger the score, the more pronounced the processing style will be. A person with a 4.5 dominant pin code will seem strong and purposeful whilst one who is 7.5 dominant will seem like a force to be reckoned with! It is helpful when you are doing an analysis to consider the gender of the person you are analysing and the processing style, especially when you consider the decade in which the person was born and how strong the 'pink box / blue box' social programming might have been at this time.

INTERPRETING THE PIN CODE

Now you have all the techniques to successfully analyse someone's birth date. It takes time to learn and remember all the different terms and techniques. Practise will make perfect. I will also take you in a step-by-step process to do this analysis; however, it is not important to follow it regimentally. The more analyses you do, the less you will rely on this prescriptive process. To practise this, take a blank analysis page from the back of the book, cover the answers below and do the calculations yourself.

We will use the birth date 2nd May 1975 for this analysis. This person is male.

Birth date: <u>2nd May 1975</u>
Male

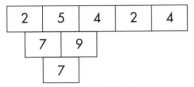

	Elements	Dominant	Passive
Air	2	0	1
Water	1	N/A	4
Fire	0	0	N/A
Earth	2	0	2
Nine	N/A	0.5	0.5
Total	N/A	0.5	7.5

7.5 Passive

Life cycle:	2	3	4	5	6	7	8	9	1
Nursery	0	1	2	3	4	5	6	7	8
Year:	1975	1976	1977	1978	1979	1980	1981	1982	1983
	2	3	4	5	6	7	8	9	1
Teenage	9	10	11	12	13	14	15	16	17
	1984	1985	1986	1987	1988	1989	1990	1991	1992
	2	3	4	5	6	7	8	9	1
Bachelor	18	19	20	21	22	23	24	25	26
	1993	1994	1995	1996	1997	1998	1999	2000	2001
	2	3	4	5	6	7	8	9	1
Nesting	27	28	29	30	31	32	33	34	35
	2002	2003	2004	2005	2006	2007	2008	2009	

Adulthood	36	37	38	39	40	41	42	43	44
Spiritual	45	46	47	48	49	50	51	52	53
Family	54	55	56	57	58	59	60	61	62
Achievement	63	64	65	66	67	68	69	70	71
Wisdom	72	And onwards							

Check you have completed the template and table correctly. Go back and reread any parts of this, or the previous chapter, if you have incorrect figures or are unsure of the calculations. It is very important you do the calculations correctly. No one will thank you for giving them an analysis that is based on incorrect information. When you are confident of the calculations and have the correct the figures, move on to the analysis.

THE ANALYSIS

Step 1: Look at the elements

You will see this man has a lot of water – four water and no fire in his Pin Code.

Some Pin Codes will have balanced elements (2 of each) and there are some which are entirely one element, like fire. The elements give you an immediate handle on this person. Our male example here will be a strongly emotional person who does not naturally have a strong drive and he doesn't like confrontation.

When one or more elements are completely missing in a Pin Code, I find that the person will not display that element in the normal course of their day. However, if their button is pushed which sets off the fire, as in this example, the person will struggle to put it out – they risk burning themselves out. No water in a Pin Code and the person will seem unemotional to others but push the wrong button and you'll have the Victoria Falls on your hands. Pin Codes with little or no air can chat away happily, but asked to express themselves verbally on an important issue and they will clam up. I suggest to these people to write down important things they want to say and they will find it a much easier form of expression.

Remember to think of the elements as you would if you experienced them in nature. A Pin Code might be all air and water – this person will be bubbly (think of the air through water). A person with lots of earth will be solid, grounded. A person with earth and fire will smoulder and can lose their passion and drive (earth puts out fire). A Pin Code with lots of air and fire will be an explosive mix.

Step 2: Check the gender and processing style.

Our example is male and his processing style is 7.5 passive. This is a strongly creative man who, to be successful, will need strong dominant energy around him. He will certainly be in touch with his feminine side. If he has been brought up in a very traditional environment he might feel constrained to express this part of himself. If he has 'permission' to do so he will happily find creative ways to express his personality.

Step 3: Look at the numbers in the Pin Code

Our man is a nurturer, his personality is a Two. In fact, he has two Twos in his Pin Code so the Two energies will be magnified. These Twos reinforce his 7.5 passive processing style. He will enjoy being the family man and will be very happy playing father to his children if he has any. He will want children, but he won't be a traditional husband – in the macho sense. He'll be happier selecting the décor than managing the family finances. Consider his inner child position – it is the child, the number Nine. He will play with the kids and just love it! In fact, he has the desire to stay the child, without all the responsibilities of adulthood, to just kick back and play.

The other immediately notable thing about this Pin Code is the two Sevens in the inner self and sense of spirit positions. This man is actually very private. He really doesn't want his private self to be public. He will work hard at keeping it this way. It will be hard to get to know this man well.

He's chattier in a social situation when he doesn't know you well and can talk on superficial topics (Five in social consciousness). He sees the world as a place of performance (Four in global consciousness). His life cycle is a Two so when change happens to him, his nurturing and caring skills will be further reinforced and he will want the best for his family.

His lesson in life is a Four. It will be important for this man to be scrupulously honest. A Four in the lesson will demand he maintains his integrity. He has another Four (in the global consciousness) so the Four energies will be stronger so the lesson greater.

Step 4: Look at the Life Stage Matrix

Our man is in a Four year in 2004 in the nesting stage. We know a Four year means change. It can be change of work, relationships, attitude to life, anything that's important to us. We either embrace change or we fight it. In a Four year, when we fight it, it tends to come back and hit us in the back of the head.

Nesting stage means building time, for home and family and career. The Four will mean he will be challenged in these arenas, so he will need to watch out for problems that might threaten the family structure or career. Of course he must stay aware of his lesson (also a Four) at this time, as the pressure may influence his integrity and honesty.

2005 is a Five year, a year of movement. Often 'movement' follows a year of change, when we can no longer hold onto the past (that bash in the back of the head usually does it for us) and we have to move forward.

2003 was a Three year for our man and Three years are intense, hard work and often result in burnout. Without any fire in his Pin Code, he will have struggled to contain his work rate and found himself tired, yet unable to stop. He will have experienced much hard work and would have hoped for some reprieve in 2004, but no, there is enormous pressure on him to make big changes. The movement will happen in 2005.

Step 4: Blend the information

This is a man who is kind, nurturing, creative and loves his family but tries to maintain a very private life. According to his Pin Code, he's very emotional and, in 2004, is facing the challenge of change.

If you keep up with celebrities and their birthdays, you might have guessed whom we have analysed. It is in fact the footballer David Beckham.

Here's another famous person's birth date for you to practise your calculation and analysis skills. Use a template from the back of the book to do your calculations and then check there are correct with the answers following on here.

The birth date to analyse is 6ᵗʰ July 1946 and the person is male.

Birth date: **6ᵗʰ July 1946**

Male

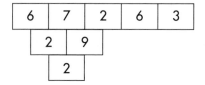

	Elements	Dominant	Passive
Air	0	0	0
Water	4	N/A	4
Fire	3	3	N/A
Earth	0	0	0
Nine	N/A	0.5	0.5
Total	N/A	3.5	4.5

4.5 passive

Life cycle:	6	7	8	9	1	2	3	4	5
Nursery	0	1	2	3	4	5	6	7	8
Year:	1946	1947	1948	1949	1950	1951	1952	1953	1954
	6	7	8	9	1	2	3	4	5
Teenage	9	10	11	12	13	14	15	16	17
	1955	1956	1957	1958	1959	1960	1961	1962	1963
	6	7	8	9	1	2	3	4	5
Bachelor	18	19	20	21	22	23	24	25	26
	1964	1965	1966	1967	1968	1969	1970	1971	1972
	6	7	8	9	1	2	3	4	5
Nesting	27	28	29	30	31	32	33	34	35
	1973	1974	1975	1976	1977	1978	1979	1980	1981

	6	7	8	9	1	2	3	4	5
Adulthood	36	37	38	39	40	41	42	43	44
	1982	1983	1984	1985	1986	1987	1988	1989	1990
	6	7	8	9	1	2	3	4	5
Spiritual	45	46	47	48	49	50	51	52	53
	1991	1992	1993	1994	1995	1996	1997	1998	1999
	6	7	8	9	1	2	3	4	5
Family	54	55	56	57	58	59	60	61	62
	2000	2001	2002	2003	2004	2005	2006	2007	2008
Achievement	63	64	65	66	67	68	69	70	71
Wisdom	72	And onwards							

Starting the analysis for this man, his Pin Code is notable for the lack of air and earth elements. With the lack of air, this can make communication, when he's put on the spot, difficult. Also he won't be particularly practical without earth in his Pin Code. He has strong water and fire elements and when we think of the elements in nature we know water puts out fire so he will be awash with emotions, one moment passionate and fiery the next he might be tearful and somber.

This man processes with 4.5 passive energy, so he will benefit from having dominant processing people around him to help make things happen.

With the two Sixes in his Pin Code he will be charismatic and charming. He will want harmony around him and will become stressed when it's lacking. He has three Twos which will make him a very caring, nurturing person. The Two in his inner self suggests he sees himself as a nurturing person even if to the outside world he seems somewhat aloof (his Seven in social consciousness). The Six in his personality and the Seven in social consciousness will create some tension in his working life. He is aloof and cool in social situations but he actually wants to connect with people in a much closer, warmer way (the Six in his personality), so he might come across as a little insincere at times.

Note that this Pin Code has no air element. This means that spontaneous conversation or making an off-the-cuff speech can be very difficult to execute. When 'put on the spot' he will not be understood and he can make many faux pas and blunders. This man needs time to move into his 'space' (finding 'air') to work out what he's going to say and when he is ready he'll come across with confidence. People who are unaware of his Pin Code may quickly judge him as being stupid, rather than appreciating that he is merely operating within his Pin Code process.

His Three lesson requires him to remain focused on the job at hand otherwise he may become distracted with too many things going on at once.

This man is in the family stage and experiencing a One life cycle year in 2004. He will be able to display strong leadership qualities in this year. When I tell you George W Bush is born on this day, you will appreciate why he will be so difficult to beat in the US presidential elections in 2004.

If you are new to the Human Pin Code, initially practise the Pin Code calculations and analysis on people whom you know. This will help you remember the elements and essences of each number because when you do the Pin Code of someone new who has for example a Three in their personality position, you will remember your sister who had a Three in the same place.

As I have said, it is very important for you to learn the essence of the numbers, the Pin Code calculations and what the positions in the Pin Code mean, as well as the elements, processing style and life stage matrix calculations. On top of all this you need to know how to analyse all of these things into a coherent reading. It may seem a lot and even somewhat overwhelming, but the more you practise the easier it becomes and using the templates, tables and matrix will make it simpler.

You will need to be competent in all aspects of analysis of an individual Pin Code before you start analysing how two Pin Codes come together in a relationship. Because Pin Codes is an exact science, when we add two Pin Codes together we can calculate the exact 'chemical' reaction between the two people. This is the exciting development of the Human Pin Code, it's called the Synergy between two people.

RELATIONSHIPS

The Human Pin Code is an exact science based on the principles of atomic physics. We can determine the 'chemical' reaction between two people by combining their Pin Codes. The combined Pin Code, or what I call the Synergy Pin Code is then analysed in combination with the two original Pin Codes. A different combination of Pin Codes can make up the same Synergy Pin Code, so it's actually three Pin Codes that we need to take into consideration in the Synergy analysis.

None of us are immune to the highs and lows of relationships; in fact relationships are an integral part of human existence. We relate to people in all aspects of our lives; with our family, in our work environment, with our friends. The highs in our relationships give us such pleasure and enjoyment, we constantly strive to achieve these. The lows give such pain and anguish that we all try to avoid the trauma, one way or other.

The whole arena of relationships can be treacherous; from meeting the right person to managing the stresses and strains. Few of us can claim not to need help in our relationships, be it with a work colleague, boss or with our difficult teenage child or beloved spouse. Now we have a tool to help us identify the strengths and weaknesses in relationships, navigate the difficult the times and take action to improve our lot.

Firstly we need to understand the process of our love relationships and, as with all things Pin Code, we have a way of looking at this process which allows us to understand why we make the choices we do.

We need to understand that humans process from an emotional perspective. We start life and relationships with needing nurturing, (love – emotion). This nurturing is expressed in words (communication – intellect), with enthusiasm (passion and drive – fire) and the most important, security – the feeling of belonging (physical or earthly connection). The physical expression of our belonging often comes in the possessions we have, such as our house, car, jewellery, etc. as a measure of our success.

We all have needs: food, comfort, security, love and our expression in verbal and physical terms, of our feelings for each other. Our spiritual needs, expressed in our emotional well being makes us whole human beings.

It is often our perception that others will fulfill some or all of these needs. Many a woman has sought a man to provide her with security whilst men look for the pretty woman to provide him with his emotional and physical needs. So often, however, as is told by our sadly increasing divorce rates, our way of finding our mate can result in disappointment and we end up with a broken heart.

In the development of the Human Pin Code I have become increasingly aware that the search for 'The One' to fulfill our needs is often a subconscious desire to balance our Pin Code. Let me give you an example of this.

Maria came to see me in a dreadful dilemma. She is a lovely woman who had endured much difficulty in her life. She told me she wanted to leave her second marriage as it had become very traumatic. Her husband was physically and verbally abusive to her. Her dilemma, as she put it to me, was, she felt compelled to stay with her second husband when she actually wanted to return to her first husband. She felt torn by this and didn't know what to do.

I calculated Maria's Pin Code:

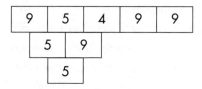

Immediately I could see that Maria lacks water or fire. The dominance of air (three Fives) and Nines (four in total), make Marie full of ideas, fun and frivolity. Her single Four (in global consciousness), struggles against the power of the other two numbers to give her much stability and practicality.

Her Synergy Pin Code with her first husband's is:

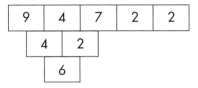

This Synergy Pin Code has four water elements, two earth and one fire element. Importantly it doesn't have any air in it which is Maria's dominant element. It was clear to me that Maria enjoyed this relationship because it brought to her access to a lot of emotional parts to which she had no access on her own. There was also more practicality with two earth elements in the Synergy Pin Code so things actually happened for her when she was with her first husband. There is a little bit of fire in the sense of spirit position, which is a nice place for a Six as it gives the relationship a warm, passionate burn from underneath.

When Maria discovered she was pregnant at first she was very excited by the prospect of having a baby but the reality of the toddler and unruly child stages became too much. She admitted she was a reluctant mother at best. I have found in my studies that women without water in their Pin Code, as in Maria's case, are often reluctant mothers. It's common for them to have a child by accident or because of pressure from their partner. And in Maria's situation, to make matters worse, her husband had not wanted children at all. The pressure of the children on their marriage (she had another in a moment of weakness, she told me, when she accidentally became pregnant with her second child) was intense. It became "the children or me" for her husband, the children won and eventually he left.

Maria's second husband's Pin Code created the following synergy:

1	2	5	8	9
	3	7		
		1		

This Synergy Pin Code has three air elements, two waters, one fire and one earth with a Nine in the position of lesson. With Maria's dominant air element, together with the Synergy Pin Code's dominant air element, there is incredible stress for her in the relationship. The two waters aren't enough to hold it together for her and she has little emotional fulfillment. In fact, the pressure became so great, she sent her children to stay with her mother as she felt the tensions were not doing them any good at all. Their departure didn't improve things much for her or the relationship but still she didn't feel she could leave him, she had this deep nagging feeling that she had to stay. All the air in their Synergy Pin Code and her Pin Code makes for an addictive situation, and as is often the case with addictions, they can become destructive.

When we are unaware of whom we are, we will subconsciously seek others to fulfill our missing aspects. Maria's first marriage gave her significantly more fulfillment than her second marriage. However, the over-riding lesson for Maria wasn't actually which husband to be with, but how to live her life happily. I described to her the potential contained in her Pin Code and, by understanding herself better, she became more tolerant of herself. Her dilemma evaporated. She could understand it wasn't about leaving one husband for another. Her task was to understand herself, to recognise that she needs to find more balance in herself.

As I've mentioned earlier, often in the teenage life stage (the stage when we develop our emotional aspects), we are not coached by our parents on how to fall in love and manage the whole romantic process.

Left in this void, we blindly connect with people who come along and lurch from one relationship to another, in a sort of haphazard way, hoping to find 'The One'.

Any emotional trauma we have experienced will also be playing out in our choice of partner. Again without any assistance in learning this process we will be lost in the mine field of confusion in relationships. Eventually we seek help for our 'damaged' feelings of disappointment, grief and anger at life and what it has done to us.

If we were told early on that the process of love needs to develop in a certain way, we might have short circuited some of our trauma. But at least we can do it now – there is no time like the present. The process of love starts by seeing someone we like and then talking with them to discover who they are. If we like what we hear, then the next stage to develop is an emotional connection. By this I mean discovering the emotional aspects of the person. How does he or she react to you and your life? How do the two of you relate when things are stressful and trying as well as when things are easy and fun? Do you like the way he responds to other drivers in the traffic? How does he relate to animals? Do you like the way she talks about her grandparents? These are all indicators of the person's emotional values.

Once you have decided the emotional connection is what you want check out their deeper values for life. Does his or her spiritual view of life resonate with yours? Can you live with the differences? What's important for you spiritually and can you share it with this person and feel supported in it?

Finally if you feel your intellectual connection, emotional bond and spiritual values are sufficiently good, then it's time to get physical!

Too often we muddle the process of love. We meet someone and quickly move to the physical. We fall in love so quickly, that we're really falling in love with love, not with the person. We don't really know the person. We don't know anything about them except a little of their mind. When lust takes over (especially in the bachelor stage), we confuse it with love. When the lust (love) fades we become disillusioned with the relationship because we have no real foundation, no emotional connection. The feelings of disappointment and pain surface once more.

Help is at hand to learn the process of love. No longer do we need to meet someone and form a bond which we think is love. No longer do we have to interpret our own feelings in isolation and then moving to trust the other with our 'heart' with no knowledge of the other. No longer will they drop our heart, breaking it because we now know how to play in the game of love and we even know the rules. The Human Pin Code is the platform on which to understand the game.

Our work and business relationships, can also can be a huge source of angst. We spend a third of our day at work, so if these relationships are working properly we will benefit from a lot less stress, more productive working environments and a happier time. Our decision to work in certain companies, with certain people, is often driven by a process we cannot control. If we are the boss, it can be advantageous to recruit more compatible team members by using the Pin Code analysis to help smooth the dynamics. However, as an employee, when we start a new job, we do not have this type of opportunity.

The Pin Code's value in this situation is to firstly understand yourself in a work environment and then look at the Synergy between you and specific co-workers. This can help you minimise any conflict and maximise the positive aspects of your working relationship.

The same goes for family dynamics. You may wonder why you've never got on with your brother or sister, or why your mother drives you demented. The Synergy Pin Code between the two of you will illuminate all stresses and strains giving you the opportunity to be more tolerant of yourself, the other person and the situation.

In fact any relationship can be analysed if you want to. It is simple to do when you know the principles of Pin Code analysis. Before you proceed to the next chapter, please refresh your memory on how the Pin Code is calculated and analysed in the previous chapters.

CALCULATING
SYNERGY PIN CODES

The basic principle of the Synergy Pin Code is the same as the individual Pin Code. It is the same eight digit matrix but instead of being derived from a birth date it comes from adding two Pin Codes together.

Let's take David Beckham's birthday, which we analysed in an earlier chapter. His birthday is 2nd May 1975 and his Pin Code is:

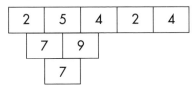

His wife, Victoria Beckham, is born on 17th April 1974 so her Pin Code calculates as follows:

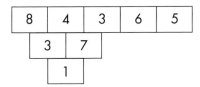

To create the Synergy Pin Code we add the two individual Pin Codes together, so we add the personality numbers together (Victoria's personality number is Eight and David's is Two so add 8 + 2 = 10, reduce the number to a single digit, 1 + 0 = 1) and put that in the first position on the Synergy Pin Code.

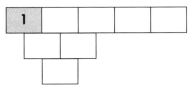

To calculate the second position, add the number from David's second position with the number in the second position from Victoria's Pin

Code: 4 + 5 = 9. Write the Nine in the second position in the Synergy Pin Code.

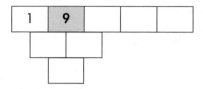

Add the numbers in the third positions 3 + 4 = 7 and write it into the third position in the Synergy Pin Code.

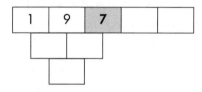

Now you can calculate the remaining numbers in one of two ways. Either you can continue to add the two numbers from the two individual Pin Codes for each position as we have been doing, or you can calculate the five other numbers in the Synergy Pin Code from the three already in there as you would for an individual Pin Code. Whichever way you do it you will end up with the following Synergy Pin Code:

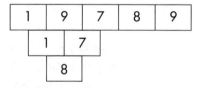

We calculate the elements and processing style of the Synergy Pin Code in the same way that we would calculate these figures for an individual Pin Code. The dominant air number is One, the passive air number is Five. All water numbers are passive and all fire numbers are dominant. The Four is the passive earth number whilst the Eight is the dominant earth number.

Remember with Nines in a Pin Code you give each Nine a score of 0.5 for Dominant and Passive energies, so in the case of this Synergy Pin

Code there are two Nines (0.5 + 0.5 = 1 for the dominant score and 0.5 + 0.5 = 1 for the passive score). Write this in each column for the Nines.

The final step is to add the numbers in the dominant and passive columns to determine the processing style.

	Elements	Dominant	Passive
Air	2	2	0
Water	2	N/A	2
Fire	0	0	N/A
Earth	2	2	0
Nine	N/A	1	1
Total	N/A	**5**	**3**

5 Dominant

This Synergy Pin Code has two air, two water and two earth elements, but no fire elements. The relationship processes with 5 dominant energy.

We will analyse this Synergy Pin Code later in the chapter.

As you do more and more of these Synergy calculations, you will become quite quick at them. It is always exciting to see the numbers unfolding and you may be tempted to make a quick judgement about the relationship as you calculate each number. Restrain yourself! Wait until you have all the aspects calculated before you attempt an analysis.

To practise calculating the Synergy Pin Code now use the birthdates 18th December 1963 for a man and 11th February 1969 for a woman and fill in a blank Synergy template from the back of the book and then check your answers against those on the next page.

Birth date: <u>18th December 1963</u>   Birth date: <u>11th February 1969</u>

Male   Female

9	3	1	4	4

3	4

7

2	2	7	2	4

4	9

4

Elements	Dominant	Passive		Elements	Dominant	Passive
1	1	0	Air	0	0	0
1	N/A	1	Water	4	N/A	4
2	2	N/A	Fire	0	0	N/A
3	0	4	Earth	3	0	3
N/A	0.5	0.5	Nine	N/A	0.5	0.5
N/A	3.5	4.5	Total	N/A	0.5	7.5

4.5 Passive   7.5 Passive

Synergy Pin Code

2	5	8	6	8

7	4

2

	Elements	Dominant	Passive
Air	1	0	1
Water	3	N/A	3
Fire	1	1	N/A
Earth	3	2	1
Nine	N/A	0	0
Total	N/A	**4**	**4**

4/4 processing style

Congratulations if you got all the calculations correct. If you had some errors, please go back to the previous chapters to refresh your memory on how to do the calculations. We do not calculate a life stage matrix with a Synergy Pin Code because often people can't remember exactly the day they met, or maybe they're not exactly sure when the relationship started – was it the day they first met, or their first date, or maybe when they knew they were in love.

As with the analysis of the individual Pin Code we follow similar steps for the analysis of the Synergy Pin Code. The analysis steps are:

Step 1 Look at the elements.

The woman in this example on the left has no air or fire elements but has strong water and earth. The man has more balanced elements but still has only one air and one water. Their Synergy has a lot of water and earth with a little air and fire. From the woman's point of view the Synergy gives her a little more balance, but not overly, as the predominant water and earth in her Pin Code is still predominant in the Synergy Pin Code. The man on the other hand, who is short of water, receives a lot of emotional support in their relationship and his earth is reinforced further. All this earth in all three Pin Codes indicates that they can be a bit stubborn and the doubling up of water for the woman could make her somewhat emotional.

Step 2 Look at the processing styles

Both the individual Pin Codes are processing with passive energy. The woman has the maximum processing style of 7.5 passive. The man is 4.5 passive. Their combined Pin Code is 4/4 which is balanced processing energy. An individual with 4/4 energy will be able to go with the flow and so will this couple. As both are passive processors, there may be difficulties in making things happen but they will feel more dynamic together with the 4/4 relationship processing and together they can create action.

I have found that the more passive a Synergy Pin Code, the more easy the intimate relationship and more likely it will have longevity. It seems that strongly dominant relationships incur such conflict that often the individuals struggle to step back from the conflict. It is important to understand that in a dominant processing relationship someone has to step back, both of you cannot be dominant so it takes a lot of effort to diffuse difficult situations.

In strongly passive relationships the conflict is more easily resolved. Either of the couple will acquiesce (it depends a little on the actual numbers in the individual Pin Codes as to who is more likely to step back). In the case of our example here the woman is more passive and she will probably acquiesce more often during an argument.

Step 3 Look at the Pin Codes

The woman in this relationship is very nurturing – triply so in fact as she has three Twos in her Pin Code (the Twos in her personality, social consciousness and life cycle). Where numbers are repeated in the Pin Code you will remember that the energies are exacerbated.

The man, whilst being 'the child' in his personality, he has two Threes, a One and a Seven along with three Fours. The close proximity of the Threes to his Nine helps the Nine behave a little! The Threes are organising and devoted with plenty of ambition and drive. The One is a leadership number and the Seven very creative.

Interestingly both have three fours in their individual Pin Codes. The number four embodies the essence of integrity and individuality. It's also dramatic, prophetic, off-beat and eccentric. The man has a four in his inner child position so he will be able to be dramatic when put on the spot.

Their Synergy Pin code is notable for the Two in the personality and the Two in the sense of spirit. They will nurture, love and care for each other. They have two Eights in the Pin Code which will make them create material things together, for example a home or a business. The

Five in the social consciousness will make them seem to others very adventurous and full of ideas.

With the Seven in the inner self and four in the inner child they will need to be careful that they maintain their honesty and integrity in the relationship. The four represents integrity and the Seven is often reserved and aloof, so the combination can be difficult. However the nurturing Twos will help enormously as they will deeply care and love each other very much.

When change happens (the Six in the life cycle position) they will work hard to ensure harmony in their relationship.

Step 4 Blend the information

This couple has a strong relationship with deep caring and love for each other. The woman may not find it as completely satisfying as it does little to balance her individual Pin Code, in fact it reinforces her emotional and practical aspects. She may need to find mental stimulation and drive and ambition through other people. The man will find the relationship very nurturing and emotionally satisfying. He is more likely to be the driver in the relationship, however neither are very pushy and tend to drift along quite happily going with the flow. During conflict it is likely that the woman will back down as she has a stronger passive processing style than the man. With all their Fours in their Pin Codes, they will enjoy being off-beat and dramatic and the Eights in their Synergy Pin Code will help them to attract money together. Outsiders will see them as adventurous and loving.

You might be interested to know who these two people are. Did you guess they were Brad Pitt and Jennifer Aniston?

To practise the analysis further we will use the earlier example of David and Victoria Beckham. Their individual Pin Codes and joint Synergy Pin Code are on the next page.

Birth date: <u>2nd May 1975</u> Birth date: <u>17th April 1974</u>

Male Female

2	5	4	2	4

7	9

9

8	4	3	6	5

3	7

1

Elements	Dominant	Passive		Elements	Dominant	Passive
1	0	1	Air	2	1	1
. 3	N/A	3	Water	1	N/A	1
0	0	N/A	Fire	3	3	N/A
2	0	2	Earth	2	1	1
N/A	1	1	Nine	N/A	0	0
N/A	1	7	Total	N/A	5	1

7 Passive 5 Dominant

Synergy Pin Code

1	9	7	8	9

1	7

8

	Elements	Dominant	Passive
Air	2	2	0
Water	2	N/A	2
Fire	0	0	N/A
Earth	2	2	0
Nine	N/A	1	1
Total	N/A	**5**	**3**

5 Dominant

Firstly let's look at the elements in the Pin Codes. David as we know has no fire in his Pin Code. He has three waters which give him a strong emotional response. Victoria on the other hand only has one water and three fire numbers. Their Synergy Pin Code however has balanced air water and earth but notably no fire. As we know in Pin Codes without a fire element, they tend to be dormant in expressing their passion and drive until their button is pressed and then it can be hard to stop them!

The processing style of David is strongly passive which is balanced by Victoria's dominant processing style. The Synergy Pin Code operates under dominant energies which may make it difficult to resolve conflict.

It is notable that their Synergy Pin Code has a One in the personality and a One in the inner self. This may make for challenging times for both parties, as the One energy is to lead. Providing one party is prepared to let the other lead it can make for a very successful partnership. The Nine in social consciousness makes outsiders see them as a fun-loving partying couple, while the Eight in sense of spirit will make for good creation of material things – their home and business together.

There is no good or bad relationship, but some relationships are easier than others. The value of doing a Synergy Pin Code is to help understand the dynamics of the relationship and appreciate how much balance each party is achieving within the relationship. It can help knowing that an aspect, for example intellectual stimulation is not being satisfied, so the person can seek it elsewhere and their partner doesn't need to feel threatened by such activity.

The value of using Pin Code Synergy in dating cannot be underestimated! It is very helpful to see how the Synergy works between two people before you even start dating. And remember to follow the process of love I outlined in the previous chapter. Often when single people yearn for 'The One' (or 'any one') we can use the

Synergy Pin Code to determine what the 'relationship contract' with a prospective date will be. The earlier you do it, the sooner you'll know what type of relationship you're entering into. You might even identify what I call your 'soul mate' which is what we'll discuss in the next chapter.

SOUL MATES
IT'S THE TWO THAT'S THE GLUE

The term 'soul mate' has become more popular in recent years. I did a search on the Internet and found many different nuances of essentially the same definition. We seem to have adopted the term 'soul mate' or 'soulmate' to mean a forever relationship or true love. Some of the proponents of the term indicate that we have soul groups from which we incarnate and when we meet these people in life we 'know' them as soul mates.

I don't support these views. I certainly don't see reincarnation as the Buddhist or New Age communities do. I see reincarnation as the transition between the nine life stages we experience in this life. As we turn nine years old we are transiting from our nursery stage to our teenage stage. It's a new life stage. The transition is a reincarnation. I encourage people to celebrate these milestones. As a child turns nine their learning experiences change from the intellectual development (the nursery life stage is an air or intellect stage) to emotional development (the teenage life stage from year 9 to 18 is a water stage). As we transit between our bachelor years to our nesting years at 27 years old we will become more interested in finding a long term partner with whom to build a life. It is often in the nesting or adult stages that people become very interested in soul mates.

Bernie came to see me, out of interest in the Human Pin Code rather than looking for a soul mate as he was 86 years old. He had experienced much of life and was very content with his lot. We chatted for a while and he told me of his marriage of 35 years to the most wonderful woman with whom he had three children. They had a very happy marriage and tragically she died suddenly in her mid 50s. Bernie's children at that time were all in their 20s and were exceedingly concerned how their father in his late 50s would cope with being suddenly widowed. Their parents had been inseparable for their 35 years of marriage and none of the children could imagine their father surviving without their mother. Often for couples who have this deep connection, when one person dies the other seems to fade in front of the family's eyes until they too pass away.

Bernie admitted to me it wasn't an easy time. He missed his wife deeply but his children's fears of his life's demise certainly didn't eventuate. After nearly three years Bernie emerged from his mourning and went on a holiday to Europe. On his return he met a woman, Hazel, who was 15 years his junior. Their relationship, even if not entirely approved of by his children because of her age, flourished.

Bernie never married Hazel. She always maintained she didn't need marriage to confirm their commitment and Bernie felt this was his compromise to ensure his children felt comfortable. Bernie and Hazel have lived very happily together for 25 years. Bernie's children came to accept that Hazel was a wonderful partner for their father.

Bernie, at 86, marvelled at how lucky he had been to have two such amazing relationships. He honestly didn't think he'd find anyone to fill the gap left by his wife as their relationship as he put it to me 'seemed perfect'. Yet he admitted almost sheepishly that he and Hazel had an even better relationship.

I was interested to see the Pin Code Synergies between Bernie and his wife and Bernie and Hazel. First I did the Synergy with his wife.

In reading a Synergy Pin Code we know to follow the steps of first looking at the elements, then look at the processing style and finally looking at the Pin Codes. Bernie and his wife had more water than average and no earth elements and a passive processing style.

I noticed there were two Twos in their Synergy Pin Code. It would make sense for such a loving and stable relationship to have these Twos – it makes for nurturing and caring between the parties.

When I did the calculations for Bernie and Hazel's Synergy I wasn't surprised to also see two Twos in their Synergy Pin Code. This Pin Code was also fairly balanced in terms of the elements and it was a passive processing style. The main difference between the two Synergy Pin Codes was the positioning of the Twos in the Pin Code and lack of Threes, which dominated Bernie and his wife's Synergy Pin Code.

Bernie and his wife   Bernie and Hazel

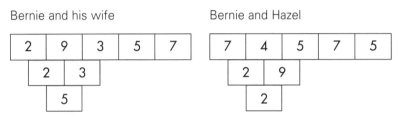

It is a helpful to understand how the positions in the Pin Code influence the relationship Synergy. The key position to note when doing an analysis is not the personality position, although it still is an important position to consider as its influence is strong. The key position is actually the sense of spirit, the number at the very bottom of the Pin Code.

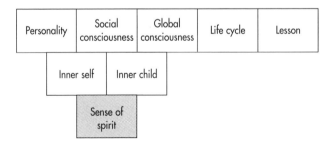

Each number's essence is listed in the addendum which will give you a full picture of the influence of the number. The position **sense of spirit** is, as we know, literally the spirit in which we do things. In the Synergy Pin Code it is the spirit in which the relationship operates.

This is a quick reference to the numbers in the position of sense of spirit in a Synergy Pin Code:

One: This is a power play. Each person will want to be the leader which can make for conflict unless one person is able to submit.

Two: The Two is the glue. This is the easiest number to have for a love relationship. It will be caring and nurturing.

Three: The Three makes for organisation. Much will happen and get done but there is not always a deep connection unless there are things happening.

Four: A tricky number is Four in this position. There can be suspicions between the two people so it's critical to be scrupulously honest and as open as possible.

Five: The Five makes for a relationship where there is lots of talk. And even more talk. It is very inspiring relationship but can tend to addictiveness.

Six: This is a passionate relationship. The couple will be very social and look great together.

Seven: A Seven in this position is a very private relationship and can be cool between the parties. Communication can also be difficult.

Eight: The Eight is an earth number and it gives a relationship a heavy feeling, almost as though there isn't enough space in the relationship. Lots of activities outdoors helps make the relationship lighter.

Nine: This is a fun, playful relationship with much forgiveness between the parties.

Whilst the sense of spirit give us a quick overview on the nature of the relationship, it's also important to look at the other numbers in the Synergy Pin Code to see how they compliment, or soften the numbers. For example you might have a Seven in the sense of spirit position but its aloofness can be modified if there is a Five in the rest of the Synergy Pin Code.

Looking back at Maria and her husbands' Pin Codes, we can have another take on their relationships by applying our new knowledge of sense of spirit. Maria was the woman who had the dilemma of being in her second marriage, unable to leave even though it was abusive and she continued to pine for her first husband.

Maria and her first husband's Synergy Pin Code is:

9	4	7	2	2

	4	2	

	6	

Not only did the Synergy Pin Code give Maria the much needed emotional connection (with all the water elements), it has a Six in the sense of spirit. It makes this relationship passionate and social. Additionally there are three Twos in the Pin Code and we know that Twos are the glue.

However, there is one amendment of which I need you to be aware. The Twos in a Synergy Pin Code will be significantly more effective in creating a loving and nurturing relationship if they are in what I call the Synergy Pin Code 'triangle'. The Synergy Pin Code 'triangle' is the six numbers of personality, social and global consciousnesses, inner self and inner child and sense of spirit. It leaves out the lifecycle and lesson numbers.

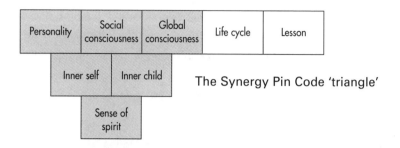

The Synergy Pin Code 'triangle'

Using the Synergy Pin Code 'triangle' we can now modify our analysis to take in to account this aspect.

As we can see from the Synergy Pin Code for Maria and her first husband on the previous page, they have three Twos in the Synergy Pin Code, but two of those are in the life cycle and lesson. They only have one Two in the Pin Code triangle in the inner child position. Twos in the lesson and life cycle position have a different meaning. We will cover the position of lesson in the next chapter. The one Two in the triangle will give them some glue.

The Synergy Pin Code for Maria and her second husband looks like this:

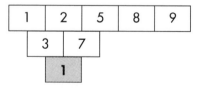

We now know that a One in the sense of spirit in a Synergy Pin Code is a power struggle. In this Synergy Pin Code there is also another One in the position of personality which will double up the effect of the One energy. The Three in the inner self position can make for a dynamic time for the couple. During stressful periods it can also make for militancy. The single Two in the social consciousness gives one Two in the Pin Code triangle. It will give some glue but it will be hard to combat the two Ones in such prominent positions.

The celebrity couples' Synergy Pin Codes we analysed in the previous chapter can also be reviewed in light of our new knowledge. Brad Pitt and Jennifer Aniston's Pin Code Synergy looks like this:

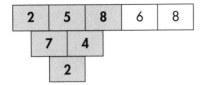

Check out their Synergy Pin Code triangle – two Twos are in the triangle and both are in important positions. One Two is in the sense of spirit position and the other is in the personality position. They will have a very loving nurturing caring relationship. Lots of glue. If problems arise, they are very likely to want to work them out to stay together.

The Beckham's Pin Code Synergy is different and poses different challenges.

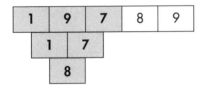

An Eight in the sense of spirit can make for heaviness in the relationship. I recommend to couples with an Eight in this position to spend lots of time outdoors. They will do well with plenty of space in their home and plenty of space in their relationship. Time apart might be effective, it's unlikely to diminish their affections for each other and can lighten the spirit.

Elizabeth Taylor and Richard Burton, Hollywood's royal couple, had a Synergy Pin Code with a Five in the sense of spirit. Inspiring and potentially addictive. It's no wonder they married, divorced and remarried.

I am regularly asked by newly dating couples to do their Synergy Pin Codes and one Synergy Pin Code which comes up quite often is one with all fire elements (Threes and Sixes) and a couple of Nines (which have no allocated element) like the following one:

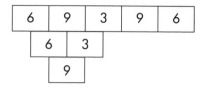

A Synergy Pin Code like this one makes for a wonderful start to dating. There is much passion and excitement and fun. It is this type of Pin Code which often short circuits the process of love. The couple with this Synergy Pin Code at the start of their relationship, unless they are aware of their Pin Codes, will be absolutely convinced it is true love. But there are a few problems they will need to deal with. One is the fact it has five fire elements. Think of it as a pile of gun-powder and one stray spark will ignite it into a huge explosion. Any conflict is likely to create an explosive situation. How the couple deals with it will depend on their individual Pin Codes. The other issue with this Synergy Pin Code is that when the passion wanes there isn't anything else to hold the couple together, there is no emotional connection between the two people. For newly dating couples with this synergy I tell them to enjoy the time while it lasts.

One couple who had this Synergy Pin Code was Prince Charles and Diana, Princess of Wales. Interestingly Prince Charles and his long time companion Camilla Parker-Bowles have a similar Synergy Pin Code. The Nines are in exactly the same place but all the fire numbers are exchanged for water numbers. For Charles and Di it was all fire (drive, passion and enthusiasm). For Charles and Camilla it is all water (emotions).

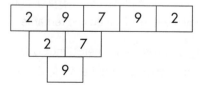

We know a Nine in the sense of spirit position of a Synergy Pin Code makes for a fun relationship, but one of the big difference between Charles and Camilla's Synergy Pin Code and Charles and Di's Synergy Pin Code, is Charles and Camilla have two Twos in their Synergy Pin Code triangle. Two is the glue. Prince Charles appears very happy with his companion and he deserves to be happy, just as everyone does.

Bernie, the octogenarian who came to see me, had a Synergy Pin Code with his wife that had a Five in the position of sense of spirit. But the two Twos were in the Pin Code triangle and in important positions – the personality and the inner self. The Twos were able to soften the organising spirit of the Threes. The Five in the sense of spirit gave them an almost addictive quality to their relationship, they were seldom apart even just for a night. It was little wonder Bernie's children were so concerned that he wouldn't survive long after his wife's death. Bernie did admit they had their clashes, but their love for each other was very strong and the conflict didn't tend to last too long. The benefit of the Threes was to help them create their family life very successfully.

Bernie and his wife   Bernie and Hazel

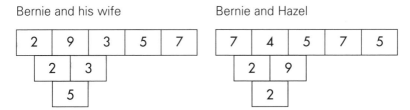

Bernie and Hazel have a Synergy Pin Code which also has two Twos in the Pin Code triangle, but they are in different positions from those of Bernie and his wife. The Two in sense of spirit makes for a deeply caring relationship – the spirit of the relationship is to love and nurture each other. Their Seven in the personality made for some coolness between them and it is not surprising that Hazel didn't need marriage to cement their commitment; she knew the commitment was already there, even with the early concerns of Bernie's children and the Seven made her happy to have a little distance. The Nine, Four and Five in the

Synergy Pin Code made for fun happy times and helped with their ability to communicate.

Through thousands of case studies, I know for sure that Two is the glue. The Two in the triangle makes for an easier intimate relationship. And the Two in the sense of spirit in the Synergy Pin Code makes for a very easy relationship. In fact, my definition of the people who have relationships with a Two in the sense of spirit is that they are "soul mates".

But having a Two in the sense of spirit doesn't automatically mean the relationship will be forever. Carmen, who was surprised when I told her that she was in a Six year both times she married, has Synergy Pin Codes with her first and second husbands that reinforce the notion that it's the whole Synergy Pin Code which needs to be considered when doing an analysis.

Carmen and husband 1   Carmen and husband 2

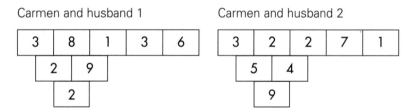

If you were only considering 'Two is the glue' in your analysis you'd immediately wonder why Carmen would leave her 'soul mate' husband number one. But the Eights and Ones in romantic Synergy Pin Codes can make the whole relationship constraining and stressful. The Eights make it heavy and the Ones create a power struggle. The relationship is also 5.5 dominant processing so when they experienced conflict it was hard for them to resolve it.

Carmen said of her first marriage that it was "easy" providing they made lots of money and did lots of things together (that's the Eight and Three operating) and they did care for each other but in a "brother / sister kind of way" (that's the Six in the lesson, we'll discover more about this in the next chapter on relationship rescue). She admitted to me that she knew her husband would never leave her (the Two is the glue) and how difficult it was for her to leave.

With her second husband she describes the relationship as happy, fun, dynamic and very loving. The Nine in the sense of spirit gives for the happy and fun times whilst the Three makes for dynamism and there are two Twos in the Synergy Pin Code triangle which makes the glue. The processing style of their Synergy Pin Code is 5.5 passive, so it's a much easier relationship in which to resolve their conflicts.

Whilst readers who are not currently in an intimate relationship can work on finding their soul mate by using the Synergy Pin Code analysis with their potential dates, it's not feasible or desirable for those already in relationships. Many relationships work without a Two in the Synergy Pin Code triangle for other reasons; including the element balance the Synergy Pin Code gives an individual. As I have said there is no good or bad relationship, just some are easier than others. Whatever is your Synergy Pin Code with your partner, by understanding your individual Pin Codes and relating them to your Synergy Pin Code, the knowledge you will gain will give you increased tolerance of yourself, your partner and your relationship. If you are experiencing a difficult period with your relationship, the Synergy Pin Code analysis will help you with relationship rescue which we will explore in the next chapter.

RELATIONSHIP RESCUE

It's important to keep in perspective that relationships work for all sorts of reasons. The Human Pin Code can help you understand the dynamics in a relationship. This understanding can be used to build on the positive and easy aspects of the relationship as well as learn how to handle the more difficult parts.

When doing a Synergy analysis, take into account all the aspects of the Synergy Pin Code. The two individual's Pin Codes must be considered in relation to the Synergy Pin Code because this is how the individual will respond to the pressures of the relationship. The same Synergy Pin Code can be created by two very different couples.

Take for example the reality celebrity couple Sharon and Ozzy Osbourne. Sharon was born on the 9th October 1952 and Ozzy's birth date is 3rd December 1948. Their Synergy Pin Code is:

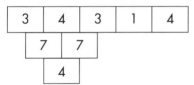

If the Olympian swimmer Mark Spitz had a relationship with singer Shakira their Synergy Pin Code would be the same as Sharon and Ozzy's. If actor Tom Arnold (who was Rosanne's husband) and Sarah Ferguson (Prince Andrew's ex-wife) became an item their Synergy Pin Code would be the same as the Osbourne's. Their birthdays are 6th March 1959 and 15th October 1959. Mark Spitz and Shakira's birthdays are 10th February 1950 and 2nd February 1977. My point here is that Ozzy and Sharon are likely to react in a very different manner to issues in their relationship, than Mark Spitz and Shakira or Tom Arnold and Sarah Ferguson because the individuals involved have different individual Pin Codes.

Individual Pin Codes bring different aspects to relationships. This makes every relationship quite unique. The Synergy Pin Code we know is your 'relationship contract'. It is the rules of your engagement. You always have choices, so if you don't like the rules of engagement, don't think you'll try to change him or her, think about changing the way you're behaving – is one or more of your Pin Code numbers operating in its reactive rather than active mode? If you really don't want that contract, you will need to find someone else.

Sometimes relationships founder because one or both partners have fixed views about their roles in the relationship. Marian and Martin were at this point when they came to see me.

Marian is a sturdy, brisk woman with lovely warm smiling eyes. Her husband of 14 years, Martin, came into the room a few steps behind her and quietly settled into his seat. I asked them for their birth dates and did the calculations. Marian couldn't wait for me to finish before she started telling me that things for them were pretty terrible and what they really needed was some help with their kids.

Martin and Marian had two sons, one eleven years old and the other eight. Two years ago the boys were both diagnosed with ADHD (Attention Deficit and Hyperactivity Disorder) and Marian had left her job as a Matron at the local hospital to be an "at home" mother. She felt if her boys had more of her attention their condition would be more easily manageable for everyone. However, it hadn't quite worked that way. Marian was very distressed that the boys' behavior seemed worse. They'd also financially got themselves into a tight fix as Martin's job as a mechanic wasn't well paying. Marian's distress was palpable. She wept with frustration at everything but, most of all, she was so distressed that her and Martin's relationship seemed at the end. It wasn't what she wanted. It also wasn't what Martin wanted.

I turned back to the Pin Codes and saw that Marian's Pin Code has a strong dominant Code, 7.5 dominant, the highest it can be! Martin's processing style was strongly passive – 6.5 passive. It was certainly a case of "opposites attract".

The problem with Marian and Martin was one of confused roles. Marian gave up her work to be the mother at home to care for her boys but it's not a natural thing for her to be only a homemaker. With her strong dominant processing she wants to be out there doing things in the world. Martin with the strong passive processing goes with whatever Marian says. During our discussion he did pipe up and say he had thought it wasn't a good idea for Marian to give up work. Marian was as quick as a flash back at him with "why didn't you say something?"

Often our upbringing has conditioned us to adopt the traditional roles for men and women. These roles were useful for our parents' generation but more and more they don't serve us well. Marian is well suited to be the bread-winner in the family and Martin is well-suited to be the nurturer in the family. When their boys were diagnosed with ADHD Marian's natural reaction was to take over and Martin went along with her. Her solution though, wasn't well suited to either of them and the resulting consequences, two years later, were not much fun for any of them.

The solution now seemed so easy to them as they sat in my office. Martin should be at home with the boys and Marian out at work. Marian did in fact go back to work and Martin resigned from his job and took up the role of fulltime homemaker looking after the boys. The boys responded brilliantly to the change and within a very short time their symptoms of ADD had diminished. I must also add that their dad kept the boys on a strict diet of no sugar including fizzy drinks, sweets and cookies.

It's quite common for women with dominant processing Pin Codes to struggle with the whole concept of homemaking. If their husband or partner has a passive processing Pin Code, it's often much better to let them be in the kitchen. If not, they will do well to find someone to help them in this arena.

When one of the attendees at a Human Pin Code workshop realised she has a dominant processing style and her husband a passive style she let out a huge squeal. She suddenly understood why her declaration, a few months earlier, that she was the woman of the house and was in charge of the kitchen, had turned into such a disaster. Her husband hadn't challenged her proclamation and she admitted how burdened she was feeling working at her job all day and rushing home to do her wifely duties.

She went straight home that evening and announced to her husband, "The kitchen is yours!" She told us the following day how delighted he was, and how relieved she was. "He always cooked such fantastic meals," she said, "I only took it over because I thought I had to, not because it was easy or fun to do. It was all about being a wife!" Her husband found cooking a pleasure that relaxed him after his hard day at the office.

As long as the woman doesn't get the domestic guilts, or the mother-in-law isn't allowed to give her judgment, it works very well, with both parties feeling fulfilled in their roles.

I have said that some relationships are easier than others and that your Synergy Pin Code is your 'relationship contract'. Often there are many reasons to stay in a difficult relationship and Sam and Ivy have a more difficult contract but choose to stay together.

The immediately noticeable thing about the Synergy Pin Code for Sam and Ivy is the Sevens in the sense of spirit position, personality and global consciousness. This makes for quite a cool relationship and the double Eight across the second row means they 'lock horns' quite regularly. Sam is dominant with strong air element and no water. Ivy is passive with no air and lots of fire. When the relationship is under pressure, Sam's modus operandi is to sulk to try to take control, while Ivy will initially shout then smoulder away with anger. Ultimately the loser would be the person who spoke first!

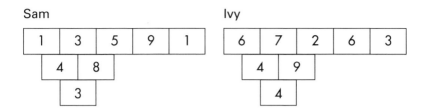

Sam

1	3	5	9	1

	4	8		

	3			

Ivy

6	7	2	6	3

	4	9		

	4			

Elements	Dominant	Passive		Elements	Dominant	Passive
3	2	1	Air	0	0	0
0	N/A	0	Water	2	N/A	2
2	2	N/A	Fire	3	3	N/A
2	1	1	Earth	2	0	2
N/A	0.5	0.5	Nine	N/A	0.5	0.5
N/A	5.5	2.5	Total	N/A	3.5	4.5

5.5 Dominant   4.5 Passive

Synergy Pin Code

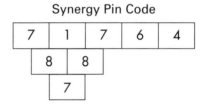

7	1	7	6	4

	8	8		

	7			

	Elements	Dominant	Passive
Air	1	1	0
Water	3	N/A	3
Fire	1	1	N/A
Earth	3	2	1
Nine	N/A	0	0
Total	N/A	4	4

4/4 processing style

You might wonder why they would choose to keep this 'relationship contract' as it is a difficult one. Sam and Ivy have been married for 20 years and remain very committed to each other, their children and family life together. Sam gets his emotional support from the relationship. Sam has no water in his Pin Code. The Synergy Pin Code has three Sevens (water elements). Ivy is attracted to Sam's intellect, his strong air element, as she has none.

With the high number of Sevens in the Synergy Pin Code, verbal communication is difficult and when they 'lock horns', they're both very stubborn. Sam wants to win and Ivy will have to climb down but this makes her feel powerless and angry. Early on in their relationship Ivy felt very frustrated that she couldn't express how she was feeling toward Sam, their arguments always ended up in extended tense silences.

One day after being exasperated about a simple little issue of who was to shop for groceries, which had exploded into two days of not speaking, Ivy wrote a note and stuck it on the fridge. "I've gone to get the milk" she wrote, "but I need your help with the baby. I'm feeling overwhelmed with everything." She stalked out to get the milk.

When Ivy returned ladened with groceries, Sam had scribbled on the bottom of the note "Sure I'll help." Ivy laughs about this now. Had they not had been in such bad space she says she might have picked another fight as to why he hadn't apologized, but at that moment any connection was certainly better than none and this simple act of alternative communication worked. It also transformed their relationship – 18 years on they still use their notes to resolve their problems.

Every relationship has the potential to fulfill each partner within its Synergy Pin Code. You just need to understand the way to do so. Whether it's an intimate relationship, friendship, siblings or work colleagues the Synergy Pin Code is what determines the way you will react to each other, commonly known as your 'chemical reaction'.

THE LESSON

In the Synergy Pin Code analyses we have done so far we have focused on the elements, processing style and the Synergy Pin Code triangle. There are two more numbers in the Synergy Pin Code which influence how the couple relates. The life cycle number operates in the same manner as it does in an individual Pin Code. However, the lesson operates in a slightly different manner and it is useful to understand its influence on a relationship.

The lesson is the number at the right end of the top line of the Pin Code

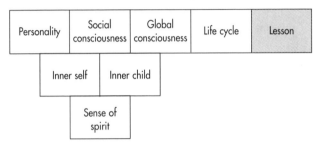

We know from the individual Pin Code analysis that the lesson is read by looking at the reactive aspects of the number. We need to minimize this reactivity to ensure the rest of our numbers are not triggered into their reactive side. A person with a One in this position will need to take care not to be temperamental, aggressive and egotistical and guard against low self esteem.

When someone is out of sorts it is often helpful for them to become aware of their lesson reactive attributes and focus on not being this way. It may seem overly simple advice but the effect can be quite dramatic as these reactive attributes can put your other numbers into their reactive attributes and then you can be sure it's difficult.

In a relationship the lesson is somewhat different from the lesson for an individual as it's the relationship that has the Synergy Pin Code lesson. When the relationship is in strife it's important to look at the lesson and see what you can do to minimise the reactivity of this number.

The meaning of the number in the lesson of a Synergy Pin Code is:

One

A couple with a One in the lesson of their Synergy Pin Code need to learn to be put first in the relationship, accepting your partner's input or participation. When one or both aren't aware they need to do this they will become despondent and the relationship potentially lethargic. Take turns each month to put your partner first. Egos will then feel stroked and the relationship will become harmonious.

Two

A Two in the lesson position of the Synergy Pin Code for an intimate relationship is a difficult lesson because your relationship is a love relationship and your lesson is a love lesson. This Two is not in the Synergy Pin Code triangle so it is not considered 'glue'. You will need to learn about loving each other. Take care not to let things turn cruel or vicious with each other; instead focus on giving love to each other. Become aware of your partner's emotional needs.

Three

The number Three is an organising, active and spirited number. A Three in the lesson position of a Synergy Pin Code requires the couple to keep focused on their relationship. The organising challenge will obstruct the real purpose of your relationship, so don't be diverted by who's way is best to do things. Keep the focus on the bigger picture.

Four

The Four is about integrity so with a Four lesson in a Synergy Pin Code think Adam, Eve and the apple. It's about temptation. Jealousy can rear its ugly head here too. Both parties will see how far they can push each other by flaunting themselves. Try to flirt with each other instead.

Five

A Five lesson in a Synergy Pin Code will push the couple to create the 'perfect' relationship, to the point of becoming highly critical of each other. Don't waste time analysing each other's faults. Remember that no relationship is perfect. Learn to plan journeys and new horizons together. You'll find that works wonderfully well.

Six

The lesson for a couple with a Six in this position in their Synergy Pin Code is to learn family values. Don't look in some-else's back yard if you get my meaning. There will be strong sexual connections. I recommend to couples with a Six in the lesson to play the 'sex bomb' and explore the physical aspects of the relationship together.

Seven

There are a number of issues with a Seven in the lesson of an intimate Synergy Pin Code. Firstly you will need to learn about embarrassment – whether you embarrass your partner or your partner embarrasses you, you need to learn how to be gentle about this. The issue of who controls the purse strings will also be prevalent in a Seven lesson. Try writing letters to each other about the money!

Eight

The Eight in the lesson for a Synergy Pin Code is all about material possessions. Be careful not to be possessive, learn to share your possessions. I highly recommend to couples with an Eight in their lesson to have an ante-nuptial agreement drawn up prior to marriage.

Nine

The Nine is such a playful number, being the essence of a child. Nine in the lesson of a Synergy Pin Code will require the couple to learn when to play and when to work. If they don't put boundaries around their play they can completely lose the plot and go overboard. Remember to create balance between work and play and try not being so stubborn.

Sam and Ivy, the couple who found leaving notes for each other on the fridge their salvation, have a Four in the lesson position of their Synergy Pin Code. Ivy told me that when they were out being social, they always ended up harmlessly flirting with other people and after all these years, she didn't feel threatened. She admitted she has been jealous, particularly early on in their marriage. When she decided to flirt a little, Sam would become very protective of her. Ivy also acknowledged she had used the tactic, at times, to get Sam's attention. I suggested the most positive thing to do in her relationship was to flirt with Sam. She giggled like a school girl!

Identifying your relationship's lesson is always helpful in the first stage of relationship rescue. When you feel your relationship is out of balance, try to observe how that lesson number is being played out and try to stop it as quickly as possible. You have to be aware of how the dynamics work between the two of you otherwise things can escalate rapidly into a crisis.

Relationship rescue can be applied to any relationship, not just intimate relationships. Whether you're having problems with a parent, child, sibling or friend, understanding the Synergy between you will help you resolve your issues and be able to move on to a happier experience. You must want to work it out together, not just feel it all comes from one side. Otherwise it becomes just that: one sided.

I had a client, Debbie, visit me and near the end of her appointment, she casually asked me about her relationships with her older sisters. Her sisters were twins and she felt the Human Pin Code didn't really fit them as they had the same Pin Code and yet to her they seemed very different. I did their Pin Codes and joint Synergy Pin Code.

Female (Twin)

1	1	2	4	5

2	3

5

Female (Twin)

1	1	2	4	5

2	3

5

Elements	Dominant	Passive		Elements	Dominant	Passive
4	2	2	Air	4	2	2
2	N/A	2	Water	2	N/A	2
1	1	N/A	Fire	1	1	N/A
13	0	1	Earth	1	0	1
N/A	0	0	Nine	N/A	0	0
N/A	3	5	Total	N/A	3	3

5 Passive   5 Passive

Synergy Pin Code

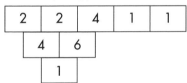

	Elements	Dominant	Passive
Air	2	2	0
Water	2	N/A	2
Fire	1	1	N/A
Earth	3	1	2
Nine	N/A	0	0
Total	N/A	4	4

4/4 processing style

For most people, it seems reasonable that two people born on the same day, with different parents, have the same Pin Codes and therefore the same basic potential but will behave in different ways. Parents, and the children's environment, will affect how the Pin Code is expressed. A child with a Seven in his or her personality position, in a household with abusive parents, is likely to become very withdrawn and aloof. A child with a Seven in his or her personality position, in a home that is very creative, will develop their creativity. The first child will still have the potential to be creative, as will the second child have the potential to be aloof.

When it comes to twins, their parents are the same and environment is often the same. Just like any Synergy Pin Code analysis, twins need to be considered in the same way. Twins in their early years are usually together most of the time, so their Synergy is played out quite intensely. In the case of Debbie's sisters they have two Twos in the Synergy Pin Code triangle so there is 'glue', but the One in the sense of spirit means they have an underlying power struggle. For them it will be difficult, they will love each other dearly and yet cause each other a lot of angst, particularly as both have Ones in their personalities. The One in the lesson adds to this pressure, as they will have internal conflict of wanting to be the leader but not wanting to put themselves first.

Debbie confirmed that this was how the twins behaved together but still they seemed quite different to her. I explained to Debbie that what I've found is that twins often display the different aspects of the numbers. Whilst one twin has the active aspect of the number (in this case a One in their personality – confident leader), the other displays the reactive aspect and for Debbie's twin sister that of low self esteem and temperamental attitude. At times the active and reactive aspects can switch between them. Twins in the adult years usually build separate lives and when they marry, their partners and the resulting Synergy Pin Code, influence the twins in different ways, so different aspects of their Pin Codes may develop and be expressed.

Debbie confirmed that the big difference between her sisters was that one was a confident leader, with a great career, and the other was very unconfident and struggled with her work. She could see that both these aspects are attributes of the number one. She also could recall times when the less confident sister did display leadership and drive, albeit in a family situation rather than at work.

I have also had triplets on whom to do Pin Code analyses. As with two people you add the individual Pin Codes together, with three you do the same thing. The analysis has to consider all three individual Pin Codes as well and the three-some Synergy Pin Code. These triplets were born on the 5th so their combined personalities were a Six (5 + 5 + 5 = 15, reduce to a single digit 1 + 5 = 6). When all three children were together they had a spirited, fun time but when only two were together and the third taken away there was a power struggle (5 + 5 = 10, reduce to a single digit 1 + 0 =1). Their mother hadn't understood why two together would always fight but when all three were playing they had a lovely time. She imagined that two playing together would be much more peaceful than all three. How wrong she was!

I recommend the Synergy analysis of more than two people to be done by a certified practitioner as it does get very complicated.

Sometimes a relationship can bring out the worst in people. It is not that the relationship is bad, it is often because the two parties don't understand each other and when in conflict they become unbalanced. Johan came to me for an analysis and I could see from his Pin Code, that along with many great attributes, he had the potential to be domineering. It's not something that I would share with someone unless they specifically asked me. Johan, a normal placid man, had recently formed a relationship with Neels. The relationship had become unhappy and things were turning sour.

I did their individual Pin Codes and their Synergy Pin Code which you will find on the next page.

Johan   Neels

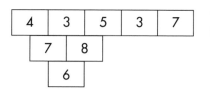

Elements	Dominant	Passive		Elements	Dominant	Passive
1	0	1	Air	4	2	2
2	N/A	2	Water	3	N/A	3
3	3	N/A	Fire	1	1	N/A
2	1	1	Earth	0	0	0
N/A	0	0	Nine	N/A	0	0
N/A	4	4	Total	N/A	3	5

4/4 Dominant / Passive   5 Passive

Synergy Pin Code

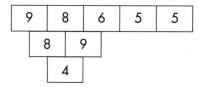

	Elements	Dominant	Passive
Air	3	0	3
Water	0	N/A	0
Fire	1	1	N/A
Earth	3	2	1
Nine	N/A	0.5	0.5
Total	N/A	3.5	4.5

4.5 Passive

Neels has four air elements and three water elements, one fire and no earth elements. He will have a very sunny, bubbly disposition. He has a passive processing style and with his two Fives (in the personality and social consciousness) he will have BIG ideas.

Johan on the other hand has only one air, two water and two earth with three fire elements and with balanced processing. His Four in his personality and two Sevens (inner self and lesson), make him a bit dramatic, in a superficial way, because he wants to keep himself private.

Their Synergy Pin Code has three air elements, and all of them are Fives. The two earths (Eights) help manage the child Nine in the personality. We know a Four in the Synergy Pin Code's sense of spirit can be difficult as there can be mistrust and suspicions between the two people. Johan's desire to keep himself private could exacerbate this for Neels.

Johan's frustration had surfaced because Neels' bright sunny self cannot make decisions easily. With all that air he'll talk and talk, have great ideas for everything but with little fire and no earth he is unlikely to act on it. If he, Neels, did make a decision he couldn't stick to it, he'd change his mind constantly until the very last minute and even then, there was still a distinct possibility that he wouldn't go through with it. Johan's way of dealing with this, prior to having any understanding of their Pin Codes, was to organize everything and ignore Neels.

This created huge frustration for Neels, as he felt his desires were invalidated by Johan 'taking over'. Neels would then nit-pick and criticize the decisions made by Johan which further inflamed Johan's temper. Sadly the frustration built to breaking point and Johan did react to Neels. It was at this point Johan knew he had to get help.

Johan saw the three Pin Codes and began to understand that Neels wasn't changing his mind to upset Johan. It was just the way Neels is. All that air in his Pin Code makes him verbally critical and Johan mustn't take it personally because it's not done to get at him. It's not personal, it's just the way Johan is.

I suggested to Johan to draw on his Four's easy going laid back attributes rather than let his fire numbers, especially the Threes, get involved. If he could step back and not make decisions for Neels and let him muddle along as he does, they will be able to go back to their fun-loving relationship.

Johan was at the brink, as was their relationship. Without the understanding of themselves, and of their relationship, they would certainly not be together. With this understanding both have said to me they have much greater tolerance of each other and now they laugh at Neels' lack of decision and nit-picking and Johan's organisation and secrecy.

The key to relationship rescue is to understand yourself, the other party and your joint Synergy Pin Code. With this knowledge you can make informed choices as to what you can do to resuscitate the relationship. You can have a long hard look at the Synergy Pin Code and decide whether it is the 'contract' you really want and then move forward to resolve the issues.

Both parties must want to work on their relationship and all relationships have a duration. It too will go through dynamics of change and the input of the two individual Pin Codes which feed the 'contract' need to know how to develop the best from it.

I've used relationship rescue for many different types of relationship, including partnerships in business. Sometimes you have the chance to look at your working relationships before you start working with someone, but often this is not the case when you're the new employee. The next chapter will give you new ways to manage your work relationships.

BIG IN BUSINESS

The use of the Human Pin Code in business has escalated. It has always had obvious uses, such as recruitment of new staff, but more and more it is being used to assist in personnel development, in making teams function in more productive and effective ways and specific conflict resolution. The application of Human Pin Code at these levels is very specialized and we have highly qualified consultants who can assist businesses in this way. Information on the Human Pin Code Corporate Services is found at the end of the book.

However, from the individual's point of view, it's all very well to sort out our love relationship but we spend at least eight hours a day, five days a week, at work, so most of us would really like to have harmonious encounters there as well. The levels of stress in the workplace have escalated in recent years and this stress often affects all other areas of our lives. Frequently a source of stress comes from difficult relationships, which tax us emotionally and intellectually, as we try to negotiate our daily tasks.

I have met many entrepreneurs whose business relationships can be a great source of delight or distress. Sometimes there's delight at the beginning and distress in the demise. I recommend that those who are planning to enter into a partnership, should, at the very least, understand the relationship dynamics. The Synergy Pin Code will give you the relationship's 'chemical reaction'. Often we overlook this in our excitement and enthusiasm in the beginning of a new venture. There is a saying "marry in haste, repent in leisure" – it can be the same in business unless you have the understanding of your relationship dynamics.

Arthur, a long-standing client of mine, came for advice as he was putting together a new business. Two people had approached him, both wanting to join him in the business. Arthur is a creative IT person, his passion is designing computer games but he knows getting them sold and distributed needs different skills from what he possesses. The first person interested in joining Arthur was a colleague from a previous company. Andrew is an extremely bright, dynamic person. Although Arthur hadn't worked closely with him he told me Andrew had an amazing track record in the industry. He felt Andrew could bring his technical skills, as well as his contacts, to do the marketing and sales job easily. He was Arthur's first choice.

Heather, on the other hand, was a personal friend of Arthur's from long ago. Whilst she had no direct experience in the IT business, she had been a successful sales person for a stationery company which had recently merged with another company. Heather had decided to take the redundancy payout and enjoy a break before looking for a new job. Arthur liked Heather but he wasn't sure she had the technical capability to adapt to the IT industry and be seen as credible. He was also uncertain of how their relationship could move from friends to business partners.

I asked Arthur for his birth date and those of Andrew and Heather and proceeded to do the Pin Code calculations.

Arthur's Pin Code is notable for its strong passive processing (7.5), the four water elements and no fire. It was very appropriate for Arthur to find a partner. He has the creative flow to make his business ideas happen, but he might not be able to hold on to them. He is well suited to be the creator but will need to be willing to give up some control of his business to his new partner.

Andrew on the other hand has a balanced processing style (4/4 passive/dominant) and three fire elements. He has the drive to make things happen. However the Three in the lesson position may make him somewhat unfocused at times.

Arthur

Andrew

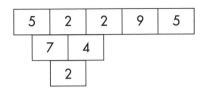

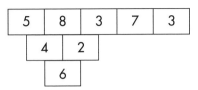

Elements	Dominant	Passive		Elements	Dominant	Passive
1	0	1	Air	4	2	2
2	N/A	2	Water	3	N/A	3
3	3	N/A	Fire	1	1	N/A
2	1	1	Earth	0	0	0
N/A	0	0	Nine	N/A	0	0
N/A	4	4	Total	N/A	3	5

7.5 Passive   4/4 Passive / Dominant

Synergy Pin Code

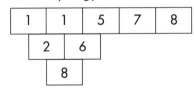

	Elements	Dominant	Passive
Air	3	2	1
Water	2	N/A	2
Fire	1	1	N/A
Earth	2	2	0
Nine	N/A	0	0
Total	N/A	5	3

5 Dominant

Both men have Fives in their personality positions which make them analytical, inventive and visionary. I could see from the Synergy Pin Code that Arthur and Andrew could attract money (the Eight in the sense of spirit) although they both would feel a weight of heaviness about the relationship as if there wasn't enough room to move. They would do well to work in different offices and communicate by email and phone. The Eight in their lesson would challenge them to share their 'possessions', which could include their knowledge and skills. The three air elements suggest there will be a lot of talk and it might be more difficult to make things happen with only one fire element.

I was mostly concerned with the Ones in the personality and social consciousness of the Synergy Pin Code. There would definitely be a power struggle between them and it could potentially play out in the public arena (one in the social consciousness), which may not be helpful for their business.

In business Synergy Pin Codes I find a more dominant processing can be helpful to make things active and dynamic. It is important however for the two parties to understand that this dominant processing will create some tension between them. One person will need to back-down when the tensions become too much. If you have a dominant processing Synergy Pin Code, try to appreciate that backing down can be a positive thing, rather than perceiving it to be a negative submission. The result of backing down allows the dynamism of the relationship to continue.

Andrew and Arthur's Synergy Pin Code have a 5 dominant processing style. Arthur will probably be the one to back-down during moments of high tension as his personal processing style is very passive. However, Andrew has the capability to back-down with his 4/4 processing style and will probably be quite reasonable about this.

Heather and Arthur's Synergy looks like this:

Arthur

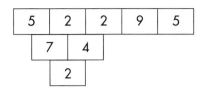

Heather

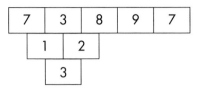

Elements	Dominant	Passive		Elements	Dominant	Passive
2	0	2	Air	1	1	0
4	N/A	4	Water	3	N/A	3
0	0	N/A	Fire	2	2	N/A
1	0	1	Earth	1	1	0
N/A	0.5	0.5	Nine	N/A	0.5	0.5
N/A	0.5	7.5	Total	N/A	4.5	3.5

7.5 Passive   4.5 Dominant

Synergy Pin Code

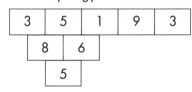

	Elements	Dominant	Passive
Air	3	1	2
Water	0	N/A	0
Fire	3	3	N/A
Earth	1	1	0
Nine	N/A	0.5	0.5
Total	N/A	5.5	2.5

5.5 Dominant

There are some similarities between the two Synergy Pin Codes of Arthur and Heather and Arthur and Andrew. Arthur and Heather's Synergy Pin Code has a dominant processing style (5.5 dominant). There are three air elements in their Synergy Pin Code and there is an Eight in the Synergy Pin Code triangle, which bodes well for attracting money.

Heather's Pin Code shows a strong organizing talent (two Threes), with a dominant processing style of 4.5. She has three water elements in her Pin Code so she will respond emotionally to events, however as two of the water elements are Sevens she will more often do this privately. She will appear somewhat aloof (the Seven in the personality).

Heather didn't have any industry experience which Arthur was concerned about. However, the One in the inner self position gives her the desire to understand and rise to the challenge of a new industry (the One's leadership trait) and the Threes in social consciousness and sense of spirit give her the motivation to do so.

The Five in the sense of spirit in the Synergy Pin Code makes the relationship between Arthur and Heather inspirational and inventive but they will need to be careful it doesn't become addictive. In business I see this addictiveness being expressed when the partners or colleagues can't see beyond what the two of them are doing and often they fail to see the bigger picture. When this is the case they can miss important opportunities by continually analysing everything.

There is another Five in the Synergy Pin Code in the position of social consciousness. To outsiders Arthur and Heather will seem inspired and inventive which will make for good business connections and may help in taking Arthur's product to market.

The Three in the personality and the Eight in the inner self of the Synergy Pin Code make for a good business relationship. Together Arthur and Heather can really make things happen and it will result in money. The three fire elements will drive their relationship and ensure it's productive and going places.

The more difficult aspect of the relationship will also come from the Three in the personality (militant and stressful) and the Three is repeated in the lesson so both of them will have to guard against taking such a position with each other. They will also need to take care not become unfocused and distracted. Additionally there is no water element in their Synergy Pin Code. This means that neither person will get any emotional support from their relationship. This is not necessarily a bad thing in business relationships (it would be more difficult in an intimate relationship) and, as both Arthur and Heather have an abundance of water in their individual Pin Codes, they're unlikely to look to this relationship to provide them with this aspect.

My advice to Arthur as to which person would be the better business partner was this: Both Andrew and Heather had attributes which would support Arthur and his business venture. Andrew also had industry experience in his favour but Heather had the ability and motivation to learn about the industry. The two Ones in the Synergy Pin Code for Arthur and Andrew would make for more difficult relations and with Arthur's strongly passive processing style, he's more likely to feel the pain of this than Andrew.

Heather's dominant processing style and the extra fire elements in the Synergy Pin Code for Arthur and Heather would create a dynamic duo, which could get a bit out of control with enthusiasm and ideas (those two Fives). Providing Arthur and Heather could keep this in perspective my recommendation was for Arthur to go into business with Heather.

Three years later Arthur and Heather still remain in business together. Arthur has told me they have experienced the inspirational, addictive aspects as well as Heather's militant bossiness but generally the business relationship has continued to work well. They are also making a great deal of money.

Another couple came to visit me who were romantically involved but wanted to go into business together. This can be a risky move because if things don't work out in the business arena it can put huge pressure on the relationship. Nathan had made a lot of money by the time he was 40 and was really in retirement mode when he met Lindiwe. She'd also been successful in her career as a creative idea's person in the advertising industry. Their idea was for Lindiwe to go out on her own and Nathan would be her business partner, financially supporting her and being an executive director of the company. Nathan admitted to me that it was really just a project he was taking on, he didn't see it as a long term thing for him.

In Nathan and Lindiwe's Pin Codes (on the page opposite) I could see that they had six air elements in this Pin Code with a little bit of fire. The fire will be fanned by this huge amount of air so it has in fact the potential to be quite dynamic. In business a Five in a Synergy Pin Code triangle inspires the two individuals and gets the creative juices flowing. Nathan and Lindiwe have three Fives so there is a great deal of creativity between them.

Both of them have sufficient fire in their individual Pin Codes to get the job done. Nathan initially took on a silent investor role, financially supporting Lindiwe until her business was fully on its feet. With his dominant processing he encouraged and supported her creativity and she blossomed. Passive processors need this type of backup and support to really relax into their talents. They have made a huge success of the business and it continues to go from strength to strength.

In understanding the dynamics of Pin Codes in business, we need to appreciate that individuals' contribution may be considered positively by some and not so positively by others.

I had a client come to me with a difficult situation. Alan is a business investor and specializes in taking underperforming businesses into very profitable operations. In this particular situation, he was in the final stages of buying into a business. He was struggling to have the incumbent General Manager to work together with him. The GM had been in the company for many years, and was extremely well respected by the workforce.

Lindiwe

Nathan

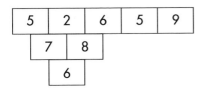

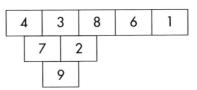

Elements	Dominant	Passive		Elements	Dominant	Passive
2	0	2	Air	1	1	0
2	N/A	2	Water	2	N/A	2
2	2	N/A	Fire	2	2	N/A
1	1	0	Earth	2	1	1
N/A	0.5	0.5	Nine	N/A	0.5	0.5
N/A	3.5	4.5	Total	N/A	4.5	3.5

4.5 Passive

4.5 Dominant

Synergy Pin Code

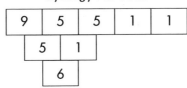

	Elements	Dominant	Passive
Air	6	3	3
Water	0	N/A	0
Fire	1	1	N/A
Earth	0	0	0
Nine	N/A	0.5	0.5
Total	N/A	4.5	3.5

4.5 Dominant

I analysed Alan and the General Manager's Pin Codes (on the page opposite). I asked Alan to describe the problems in more detail. He told me that in the beginning of the relationship, when he approached the company the GM was very excited about having a new investor. He had been very open with everything and he seemed very supportive of the investment. As time passed and the deal came closer to completion Alan was struggling to get access to anyone in the company other than the GM. When he did they were uncooperative and he suspected there was something going on.

To gain a better perspective of the staff situation Alan had met with the union representatives who were more open with him. They were also very supportive of the GM, explaining how loyal the staff were to the GM. Alan was exasperated with the situation – it all seemed so positive and yet he couldn't break into what he felt was the real heart of the company – the people.

When I looked at the Pin Codes and I could see the Synergy Pin Code of the two men made for a very difficult relationship. The One in the sense of spirit position immediately indicates there is a power play between them. The two Sevens in the Synergy Pin Code triangle suggest an aloofness or even secretiveness between the two men. They won't be able to communicate easily. The two Threes in the triangle make for at best a well organized dynamic duo but in a difficult situation such as this it can result in a controlling and militant relationship. The Nine in the social consciousness gave them a sense of friendliness and fun when they first met. It is also how others see them; playful.

The GM's Pin Code is notable for the Eights in the personality, inner child and sense of spirit. The Eight in its active role is patient, supportive and diligent and in its reactive role tends to insecurity and manipulative victimization. The Eight is repeated three times in the Pin Code so its effect will be magnified three-fold. I felt it was very possible for the GM to be operating in the reactive side of the number in this situation.

Alan

GM

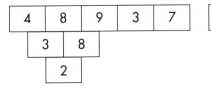

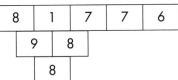

Elements	Dominant	Passive		Elements	Dominant	Passive
0	0	0	Air	1	1	0
2	N/A	2	Water	2	N/A	2
2	2	N/A	Fire	1	1	N/A
3	2	1	Earth	3	3	0
N/A	0.5	0.5	Nine	N/A	0.5	0.5
N/A	4.5	3.5	Total	N/A	5.5	2.5

4.5 Dominant   5.5 Dominant

Synergy Pin Code

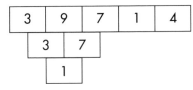

	Elements	Dominant	Passive
Air	2	2	0
Water	2	N/A	2
Fire	2	2	N/A
Earth	1	0	1
Nine	N/A	0.5	0.5
Total	N/A	4.5	3.5

4.5 Dominant

Alan felt that the GM was busy trying to control the situation and the GM with all those Eights will have a tendency to do this. Alan felt he was doing this by telling the staff one thing and him another. The GM was making the staff hostile to the investment.

Because the Synergy Pin Code was so difficult for any movement in a positive direction, one of the men would have to back-down. Both men process with dominant energy and both have three earth elements; the GM's all being Eights and Alan's being two Eights and a Four. It would be difficult for either of them to backdown. My recommendation was to either remove the GM or not to continue with the business.

The GM had always played the paternal role as a boss and the staff repaid him with tremendous loyalty. It was this loyalty and dedication from the staff that made the business investment so interesting. The staff saw the GM's behavior as very positive. Alan saw it as very negative.

Most of us have to work for or with someone and often we have little or no control over who that is. It can be very frustrating, to know how to use the Synergy Pin Code analysis and discover you don't like the 'relationship contract', when you can't always affect the outcome like Alan could – he didn't do the deal.

In general, people with a dominant processing style make for an easier boss than those with a passive processing style. A dominant boss makes for a positive boss and there tends to be few politics and rarely will there be a power play. Even if an employee has a stronger dominant processing, because the boss is in a superior position the dominant employee will back down. A passive processing employee will usually find a dominant processing boss very supportive.

If you have a passive processing style and are a boss, be careful not to become territorial or try to suppress your employee's potential. This type of behavior will make you extremely disliked because you're using your power status to do this rather than any personal power. You need to be aware that you might be stifling your team rather than motivating them.

The clever move for a passive processing style boss is to identify the dominant processing team members and make them perform so well that you look good. Try hard not to feel insecure as your team flourishes and perform brilliantly. Your staff will feel better and you can bask in their reflected glory because you will be the one who identified them as having the talent and supporting them to successfully complete the work.

Remember it's not a gender issue, it's a processing style issue. Some Pin Codes are dominant in their processing, others are passive and then there are the balanced 4/4 dominant / passive processors. If your boss is a passive processing boss and doesn't have the awareness of what he or she is actually doing and if you're frustrated beyond belief, remember you won't change them, it is the way they are. We all have choices and one of the choices you can make is to find a new job.

Many business and bosses have benefited from using the Human Pin Code to identify team problems, from having the wrong person in the wrong job, to teams of the wrong processing style. When there is the right balance of processing, elements and numbers, the group of individuals will produce what is needed. When there is instability in the processing, lack of balance in the elements and conflict with the numbers, the group's energy will be dissipated into politicking and avoidance tactics.

The skill required to analyse businesses and teams is well beyond the scope of this book. Consultants are available to assist companies in these areas and contact details are provided in the back of the book.

IN THE END

I am always delighted and encouraged when people find the use of the Human Pin Code beneficial to their lives. Romantic liaisons can be seen for what they are. Relationships can be rescued. Prospective dates can be assessed for long term suitability. Business partners can be selected for the right reasons.

With this tool, which gives such insight into human behavior instead of holding onto injustices and anger, we can look into the Pin Code to see why the conflict and tension is present. We all have choices and we can use those choices to make our lives happy if we wish to.

There are four givens in life: death, taxes, trauma and change of perception. As members of the human species we will be subjected to these givens. It is also our choice how we deal with these givens and in particular change. To understand the dynamics of the psychological mind, we need a map. The Human Pin Code is just the first step to mapping the psychological mind. It is the language of numbers common to every human being. It does not discriminate as it does not recognize culture, colour or creed.

Take a good look at who you really are, how you process and what impact you have toward others, then you will know yourself. When you can accept this, you will live your truth.

Ronelle, a successful sculptor, came for an analysis. I could see from her Pin Code she was a woman with tremendous creative talent. She had been with her partner for 12 years and now she was frustrated and at her wits end. She felt undervalued, although she acknowledged to me she gave willingly in the relationship. Her partner, Garth, was very content and didn't see any need to make any changes.

When she understood her Pin Code she appreciated that she needed to take back her power and reassure herself in the relationship. The only way she felt she could do this was to get some space between them so she could 'find herself'. She moved all her sculptures into a store room in one of the outbuildings at their home and went to stay in a friend's cottage. Tragically, the evening after she left their home was burnt to the ground by an electrical fault. Only the outbuilding remained, and Ronelle's sculptures safely stored.

The shock and panic eventually subsided and the insurance company agreed to pay to rebuild the house. In the meantime Garth was homeless. Ronelle 'took him in' to her cottage and, immediately, their relationship improved. The reason for this was a shift in the balance of power. No longer was Ronelle feeling subservient in the relationship. Garth also had the sudden realisation how much he'd taken Ronelle for granted and he couldn't do enough to make sure she was happy.

Ronelle's understanding of herself had created such an extraordinary shift in her relationship with Garth (and circumstances had in their own extraordinary way supported this shift).

Each Pin Code will interpret the same experience differently. The experience will be stored in the mind from its particular perspective. For trauma experiences the body may have healed but our mind may replay and relive the experience over and over. Unfortunately we become trapped by fear and as long as we have fear, the experiences can be relived through the mind, replayed time and again, creating a prison for our mind in our body. It's not the physical experience that's repeating, it's the mind repeating the experience. By separating the two you set yourself free.

The mind has the capacity, through choice, to set itself free to seek new experiences. The miracle of regeneration of the body will continue without your mind. Choosing to be your true self by understanding your potential through using the Human Pin Code will give you enormous freedom.

Tessa is a recent client of mine who came when her love life was nearing terminal collapse. She was devastated, as she loved this man very deeply. "What is wrong with me?" she asked. When I analysed their individual Pin Codes and Synergy Pin Code, Tessa's struggle became clear to me.

Tessa has a Pin Code of six air numbers (three Fives and three Ones) with a Four and a Nine. Tessa processes almost entirely with her intellect. Her boyfriend, with water and fire elements dominant and only one air element, was feeling completely demented by Tessa constantly analysing their relationship. She talked at him non-stop and he would then explode (all the fire). Their Synergy Pin Code triangle has a Two (some glue) but it also has two Eights in the triangle, one of which is at the bottom in the sense of spirit. This would put them at loggerheads with each other.

"You talk a lot with him don't you?" I asked. She sighed, "Yes I do but I don't mean to go on and on. I can stop talking, you know. I can sit with my daughter quite happily and not talk. But when I'm with Bill... well I just seem to get out of control and can't stop."

I asked for Tessa's daughter's birthday and looked at the Synergy between mother and daughter. Sure enough the Pin Code was full of Nines and Sevens! Tessa didn't feel the need to talk when she was with her daughter, she felt completely relaxed when they were together.

I explained to Tessa that every relationship gives us something different. With her boyfriend she exacerbated her air elements and with her daughter they were calmed. Her realisation at that moment exploded out of her, "You're saying it's not me, it's actually the 'us'. It's the relationship that triggers me to do things?" It was an important realisation as Tessa could see the 'us' or the Synergy Pin Code is what drives her behaviour, what creates proactive or reactive actions. With this awareness she was better able to choose whether she talked incessantly or not with her boyfriend.

The depth and breadth of the Human Pin Code is expanding as it is being used in more and more different situations. I am currently putting together a study of children's development, which will assist parents and teachers in understanding the behavior dynamics of their children and teenagers. I have also an exciting discovery on what creates homosexuality.

The value of understanding our Pin Code and our relationships Pin Codes shouldn't be underestimated. With knowledge and understanding comes acceptance. When we accept ourselves for who we are and others for who they are the racial, cultural and societal intolerances fall away and we can live in much greater harmony.

HUMAN PIN CODE

ADDENDUM

THE NUMBERS

The essence of each of the numbers has been taken from the Human Pin Code: The Sacred Maths in your Birthdate and updated with the new concepts from the chapter on Level 2 Principles. Those readers who have read the first book will note some minor changes to the names of the numbers. I've done this to refine the Human Pin Code as I feel these new words better relfect the numbers. It is included here for your reference.

ONE — THE CREATOR

One is associated with the element 'air'.
One is a dominant processing number.

ACTIVE	REACTIVE
leader	temperamental
airy	loud
bright	aggressive
tactile	irritable
jolly	intolerant
creative	grumpy
proud	low self esteem
assertive	lethargic
enthusiastic	depressive
talkative	egotistical
confident	mumbling

ONE represents the Creator. It is the starting basis for all numbers. It therefore goes hand-in-hand with leadership. The traits of this number include a strong sense of self worth, and an inclination towards egocentricity, originality and creativity. If you try to contain them, they often become morose, as they must have freedom of movement. One people are strongly affected by their surroundings, and need to have their egos stroked from time to time.

The person who is creating the most noise, or talking up a storm, will usually be a ONE. Watch the hands – from a distance – it looks like a new dance routine. The eyes are sparkling and seem to 'dance' as much as the hands, while the hair is usually beautiful and 'in place', be it long or short.

ONES dislike criticism, as they often feel that it challenges their authority, and they organize everything around them in such a way as to enable them to achieve maximum respect and adoration. If they fail to achieve this, they will often insist on respect – and are usually successful when demanding it. The ONE'S vibrant, creative energy is quite sweeping, and less expressive people are often swept along by the tide of enthusiasm and excitement it creates. This energy will assist a number One in rising to a position of authority. They will be firm on being looked up to by friends, relatives and even their boss – if they are not the boss already.

ONE people are extremely controlling and like to have their orders carried out, but they will protect the weak, defend the helpless, and take charge of others – provided that their instructions are followed. ONES have an air of superiority, and the head is usually held upright in a rather regal manner. They will often consider their opinions to be superior, if not flawless. Being right most of the time, others often find them annoying – especially when receiving the famous "I told you so" lecture.

Number ONES shine at genuine appreciation, but do not try to flatter them. Even though they receive your flattery with what may seem like appreciation, they will detect it instantly and think less of you for it. Their most vulnerable area is their pride – wound this, and all their virtues fly out of the window. To put it mildly… they can be most unpleasant! They are, however, very forgiving people, but you had better show genuine remorse at an offence and be prepared to grovel. Once their ego has been satisfied they will generously restore you to grace and favour – after which you will be dismissed with a stately nod, or a regal flick of the hand and a smile.

With a number One person by your side you can't go wrong – provided they are leading the way of course! At least the journey should be fun. A note of caution: a number One person is inclined to need energy when his has expired, which means he can become demanding in his attempts to draw energy off you. If this does happen, let him down gently, without harming his ego. His security will soon be re-established, and he will lift himself up again. When he is depleted, rather try and sidestep his demands and he'll soon be back on track – without your help – and with your energy still intact.

When his grumpy, intolerant side is showing, don't try and resist or fight a number One using his own methods, you will most likely come off second best. In such instances, rather harness the Active side of your own personality and access those virtues that would best soothe a worked up number ONE.

They love the social limelight, but because their Element is AIR, they have quick tempers and can even become violent. They can be dangerous if ignored. Acknowledge them when they are in a fury, and let the storm pass. Like a storm, they must have freedom to move. When thwarted, ONES become sullen and mope, but it soon passes. They get frustrated easily but, ironically, they make excellent teachers. They are also often natural sales people, communicators and designers.

Two – The Nurturer

Two is associated with the element 'water'.
Two is a passive processing number.

ACTIVE	REACTIVE
nurturing	emotional
caring	tearful
quiet	defensive
observant	withdrawn
cool	protective

timid	stormy
stable	irrational
homely	sensitive
domestic	gloomy
social	sullen
reserved	moody

Remember that person at the party, sitting in the corner minding her own business? A gentle smile from time to time, legs pulled tightly together and the shoulders slightly drooped (after all, they carry the burdens of the world on their shoulders). She was probably a TWO.

The number TWO represents parenthood; offspring; sensitivity; moodiness; caring and nurturing. So a TWO person tends to hold marriage or union in high regard; is usually married or has a partner of sorts; or is just getting over a rather painful separation.

You can easily recognise them by their big, soft, gentle, puppy dog eyes. TWOS have a strong sense of fear, and this can develop into a protective instinct, whereby they become very sensitive to nuances of any description. In other words, their intuitive nature can 'pick up vibes'. TWOS are romantic at heart, but they fear loss of any sort – loss of love, property, money, friendship or even employment. They fear the loss of those close to them, and even other people, through death or any kind of separation. Of course, we all fear loss from time to time, but with a number TWO, this feeling is far more intense than in others. For this reason, no matter how much they enjoy travelling, they always need a 'base' to return to. They are fanatically involved with their parents and family – be it for 'better' or for 'worse'.

The nurturing nature of TWOS makes them wonderful parents, but they can have a tendency to over-mother. They will hover around those they care about with words like, "Don't catch a cold", "Careful not to squander your money" or "Keep your leftovers in the refrigerator".

They can often tend to withdraw, which appears to others as if they are sulking. But if you need them to leave the security of their seat at the party, just mention that you need help with the catering, and you'll see an instant sparkle in their eyes. Now you are talking their language – the need to mother through sustenance.

The insecure side of TWOS drives them to create money, and these are some of the catch phrases that might be used by this maternal number: " Money is security", "Waste not, want not", or "A bird in the hand is worth two in the bush". And don't be surprised if they have more than one residence – just to be safe.

Number TWO people are usually extremely cautious, and dislike reckless gambling or risking their assets on a questionable venture. They believe that money should be accumulated in a safe and stable manner. They tend to keep their money in a savings account, in a safe at home, or in a 'no-strings-attached' investment. No horse racing or similar financial adrenaline pump for a number TWO!

Due to the fact that they are so cautious, TWOS appear to be secretive, and play things 'close to the chest'. They seldom let on as to their next move, and this creates a surprise when they finally reveal their secret agenda. Even though they need their security, TWOS are reluctant to accept charity from anyone as they are fiercely independent about their money. They will certainly help with a charity drive, but will not accept assistance themselves – unless they are completely without resources (which is highly unlikely). To a number TWO, accepting charity is admitting failure – a cardinal sin.

Very often, a number TWO person will become paranoid about security, or become over involved in the lives of their loved ones. They tend to hold on for too long or, with the intention of keeping others safe and warm – they can smother their 'brood'. So TWOS must be wary of possessiveness – this can often become paranoia.

Number TWOS have excellent imaginations, are incredibly adaptable, and are extremely intuitive. These talents are best expressed when the number TWO learns to 'let go' a little. They can nurture; provide for others; and love abundantly, but they must realise that they cannot live other people's lives for them. Often they need to learn that it is important for them to direct some of this love towards themselves as well.

Due to their maternal instincts, number TWOS are fiercely protective and can be extremely aggressive and volatile if their security, or that of their family, is threatened. They will not think twice about striking where it hurts, or going straight for the jugular vein in defence of their loved ones. And this is not only figuratively speaking. To get some idea of this instinct, imagine confronting a lioness with her cubs, or a herd of elephants with a calf. Run!

THREE — THE ORGANISER

Three is associated with the element 'fire'.
Three is a dominant processing number.

ACTIVE	REACTIVE
organized	misguided
devoted	hostile
independent	fierce
optimistic	fanatical
religious / esoteric	defiant
vivacious	attitude problem
candid	sulky
animal lover	indifferent
ambitious	regimented
serious	frivolous

Do you have a 21st birthday party or a wedding reception to organize, and you don't know whom you can rely on? Well, just call in a person who is a number THREE. This is the military number, the organizer, and the paragon of efficiency. However, I feel very sorry for the staff that will have to work under such a person – they would find it very difficult, unless they are used to dealing with a sergeant major. Better get some training in the army before you work for a number THREE.

Due to their quest for Truth, number THREES' beliefs form a very important part of their lives, and they will have firm attitudes about their spirituality. They will be agnostic, atheist, or deeply committed to some form of religious, or esoteric, belief. But they also tend to look on the bright side of life, much like Mary Poppins – after all, the world got this far because of their amazing organizing abilities!

You can recognise a number THREE the minute they walk into a room, as they have a quiet, yet commanding presence, which turns heads automatically. Do not get this confused with an inflated ego, even though this energy can sometimes be threatening to 'lesser mortals'. It's the type of energy that rubs people up the wrong way, just when they were feeling comfortable. THREES will not ask for praise, even though they usually richly deserve it, as they simply 'do the job well' for the sake of it, and that is all. Give them a document, and they will analyse the intention of every word, while others are still confused by its sub-title.

THREES possess an uncanny ability for seeing the end result of a project, before they even get there. This causes them to be rather impatient with slower thinking individuals. "Why can't you see? It's so obvious!" are words that most number THREES will blurt out with frustration. For this reason, most of the world's greatest strategists have a number THREE somewhere in their Pin Code. They are blunt when speaking to people, and candid to a fault. They have a genuine love for animals, and tend to defend the human underdog with the same passion and energy they display to the four-legged variety.

THREES love gambling and taking chances, and will bet on almost anything. Their bubbling optimism can be most contagious, or very threatening, depending on the attitude of the other person, but THREES should take care not to be frivolous or silly. They make excellent armchair lawyers, and they often need to be, because most of their dreams are very ambitious. One of their greatest drawbacks is their belief that they are right, and for this they are prepared to fight to the bitter end.

THREES can be very tenacious in their convictions – whether admirable or misguided. This often confuses and annoys people who do not understand them, so THREES often make enemies due to their unyieldingly high principles and personal morality. They expect others to believe in, and adhere to their convictions, as strongly as they do themselves. THREES will not compromise – so don't even bother trying to change their beliefs, to which they are truly devoted and which they believe are correct.

Four – The Investigator

Four is associated with the element 'earth'.
Four is a passive processing number.

ACTIVE	REACTIVE
individual	cryptic
enigmatic	eccentric
eccentric / different	uses shock speech
deliberate / purposeful	unconventional
loyal	vengeful
off-beat	excitable
prophetic	tactless
'live and let live' attitudes	prejudiced
perceptive	unpredictable
just	deceitful
revolutionary	fixed
dramatic	lies

Number FOUR people work to uncover the truth. If they ever suspect you of having a devious thought – beware! They are highly perceptive and will uncover harboured thoughts that do not seem moral or just. They will also tell you to your face, often without any tact, exactly what they think of you. If you attempt to hide a wrong from them, they will leave no stone unturned until they have discovered the truth. They will even twist facts to try and trap you, and you will eventually be found out.

Have you ever noticed the two masks used for the theatre? One slightly covers the other, and one is smiling while the other is tragic. This is a perfect symbol for the number FOUR. The energy of this number can slip from sadness to happiness at a moments notice. All people born as FOURS, or who have a Four somewhere in their Pin Code, will carry this energy. FOUR is the actor, the person who is able to stand on stage and deliver the most riveting of performances, yet deep under the make-up, the glitz and glamour, they could be hiding the saddest heart. Every interaction they have with another human being is a performance on the stage of their life.

FOURS seem to be elusive, and one can never quite 'pin them down'. For this reason, they can also be described as a photograph – you can see a photo in either the negative, or the processed positive – the picture could be black and white, or bursting with glorious colour. As you can see from their longer-than-average list of ACTIVE and REACTIVE attributes, they are difficult to identify. FOURS are enigmas who are often not well understood by friends and family, let alone strangers.

Because of their contradictory natures, FOURS tend to make their own rules, and their actions and words can easily shock the people around them. This is often due to the sudden change in character – the 'off-stage' and the 'on-stage' personalities. They will even deliberately try to astonish others, by doing exactly the opposite of what is expected of them. Watch their eyes carefully if you wish to identify them as being number FOUR, and you'll notice that they tend to be rather shifty-eyed, as if summing up an audience. Sadly, this is often misinterpreted as deviousness, whereas nothing could be further from the truth.

The actions of a FOUR can be larger than life. They could sweep into a room, taking over the space in an incredibly eccentric fashion – carefully designed to attract attention. Marked individuality colours every aspect of a FOUR'S nature, thoughts and actions. If there is a different way of doing something, a FOUR will discover it.

FOURS sometimes adopt strange eccentricities from a previous era, like perhaps an unusual manner of speech, or by using seriously out-dated phrases. If they are pleased with the reaction it creates, they will continue to use it. The person who says "Old Bean" and "Dear Boy", or a nasal and elongated "Daaaaarling", is often a number FOUR. The use of paradox is another clue. They love expressions like, "The only way to know what good is, is to be thoroughly evil". The more unfashionable the phrase is – or shocking the statement – the better.

FOURS are capable of living in the future with their 'way out' ideas. Whatever can be perceived in the human mind, a number FOUR can make a reality. This could range from a new-look political campaign, to a state of the art high-tech space rocket. The best way to get a number FOUR to do something, is to tell him it can't be done. Tell him that history has proven it to be impossible, and that it never has and never will be possible. You can be assured that he will get it right – just to prove you, and humanity itself, wrong. Yet, trying to get them to change something in their own lives, and you sit with 'mission impossible'. They are very fixed and stubborn when it comes to their own affairs.

You have to accept that lifestyles of FOURS range from the unconventional to the bizarre. To them, you are the freak. And they won't be too shy to tell you that either! This makes them seem prejudiced at times. But prophets were seldom recognized in their own time. And so it is with number FOURS, whose ideas and visions are often ridiculed or ignored. Secretly, they would like nothing better than to be whisked off into space or to live on the end of a rainbow – this would remove them from the humdrum and chaos of the world.

The maverick side of the FOUR often sees them joining reformist movements, or any organization that will transform, or shake up, human ideals and thinking. They have a very strong sense of responsibility, and a very clear idea of their ability to choose between 'good' and 'evil'. They understand both, and for this reason, can become deceivers of mankind. Whatever route they choose – whether 'good' or 'bad' – they tend to reach the top.

Money means very little to FOURS, and they can mix with kings and paupers with equal ease. They don't notice their surroundings – living in a tent, a van, or a mansion, is all the same to them. Their motto is 'live and let live', and they couldn't give a damn about what opinions you hold. You can say what you like, in any way you wish, it just doesn't matter. But try to change them or force your values onto them, and you'll find out just how much it really does matter!

Five — The Analyst

Five is associated with the element 'air'.
Five is passive processing number.

ACTIVE	REACTIVE
courteous	rebellious
humorous	restless
extroverted	critical
analytical	sharp-tongued
intellectual	intense
likes seeing results	volatile
enjoys change / is flexible	stressed

chatty

difficult

unemotional

contrary

logical

nervous

"You exhaust me!" is what a peace loving, tranquil person might exclaim upon getting to know a number FIVE. They are always on the move, both physically and mentally. They cannot sit still for an instant, and will often play practical jokes on innocent victims in order to relieve boredom. Their humour is often very odd (to say the least), and the improvised voice on the telephone pretending to be a homicidal maniac or 'the taxman' coming to collect, is bound to be a number FIVE.

Number FIVES have the ability to seize any situation in a nanosecond, and to turn it around completely. They do this with lightening thought and an equally fast tongue, barely giving you a chance to breathe if you engage in an argument with them. Only people with a number FIVE somewhere in their Pin Code, or numbers that have similar traits of quickness – like a ONE, can keep up with a FIVE. They have fantastical imaginations that invent the most flowery, impossible stories – but they tell them with such insistence and conviction that you are carried away, if not by truth, then by their sheer enthusiasm. But you would be lucky if you got a word in edgeways.

To calm a number FIVE down is almost impossible, which is why you will often find them at home on the stock market floors of the world. Their quick minds crave excitement; they thrive on nervous energy; are very often inventive, yet can also be very impulsive. FIVES have a keen sense of new ideas and inventions, and are more than willing to take risks based on these intuitive feelings. They are born adrenalin junkies and love sport.

Writing, advertising, communications of any kind, teaching, public relations and the many stresses and deadlines of publishing, all appeal to the number FIVE. But as this number represents communication, intellect, movement and tension, it can often lead to burnout or nervous conditions. FIVE is therefore associated with highly-strung people, and you can actually hear the nervous energy when they speak. FIVES also tend to move or travel a lot, as the number is associated with the Gypsy.

FIVES must be allowed to express their intellects, by either the written or the spoken word. They are very quick to spot mistakes and will not hesitate in pointing them out to you. Then they will analyse them to death, from every possible angle, until they are sure that the reason for the mistake is understood and will never occur again – or until the recipient of the lecture explodes. They are incapable of ignoring mistakes, even in themselves.

Change is very necessary for the number FIVE, and they crave information, even at the risk of causing an overload. Psychology, sociology, theology, politics, philosophy, physiology and almost anything intellectual will fascinate a FIVE. But they also possess strong intuitive feelings, because FIVE is an AIR sign.

Because they have logical minds, FIVES tend to rationalise their feelings, instead of trusting them. They ask "Why?" when they should simply be saying, "Yes". Their intense behaviour and attention to detail can often wear other people out, and this can lead to break-ups in relationships and friendships. They often need to get in touch with their feelings, rather than seek the logic in every matter.

If one can bear the intense electric energy and constant wacky humour of the FIVE, and if you can pin him down for long enough, you might discover an unusual sensitivity. The sensitivity will have been well thought out and pondered over, not a fake or over-romanticised, but a genuine understanding of the suffering of others and a deep-felt empathy which is rare. But you need to take the time to 'tune in' to that mad, almost intolerable frequency of his.

Number FIVES possess a wonderful charm. If you wish to sell snow to an Eskimo, a number FIVE can do it for you – they make excellent sales people. They also love people and usually have many friends, and due to their travelling habits, this means anywhere on the globe. Need a contact in a foreign land? Just ask a number FIVE.

You can always rely upon a number FIVE to be up to date with what is going on in the world. They are continuously gathering information, and the Internet is a marvellous tool for this – when they actually sit down for a few minutes. In their quest to gather information, they are constantly on the move. They might spend five minutes in front of a television set, before becoming bored – unless it is action or sport they are watching.

FIVES are keen on sports activities, as this releases their pent-up energies, and of course, these sports include bungee-jumping, motor racing and climbing Mount Everest. Their sense of adventure is insatiable, and routine or office work can frustrate them and make them ineffective. They will always be exploring some new religion or belief – not necessarily to practice themselves, but simply to analyse it. The inquiring mind of the FIVE will always have someone, or something, under his mental microscope.

Six – The Charmer

Six is associated with the element 'fire'.
Six is a dominant processing number.

ACTIVE	REACTIVE
charming	illusionary
compassionate	calculating
romantic	sentimental
sexual	self-absorbed
harmonious	discordant
sensual	demanding

affectionate	extravagant
friendly	withdrawn
good negotiator	stingy
tranquil	jealous

Number SIX people are dominated by the Element FIRE, and stand for balance, harmony and sensual love. SIX accentuates the feminine aspects of the 'fire people', being compassionate, romantic, sociable and usually very refined. SIXES have a strong social, interactive need, and when they enter a room, it is with style and panache. They always look immaculate, well groomed and dressed for the part. You may even see a SIX person busy in the garden, digging away in the dirt, but wearing a flamboyant hat and gardener's 'suit'. They genuinely love nature, especially plants and well-kept gardens, so if you want to make a number SIXES happy, take them to live in the country, or on a farm. They are meticulous and won't go into public with their hair or clothes out of place, and they always smile – you never know, a stray photographer may be lurking somewhere!

SIXES gush with personality and everyone is their friend. Charisma is their middle name and, like the chameleon, they will attach themselves to a variety of different people, and easily adapt to another's style or pose. They are not copycats, but like to make others feel at ease by adopting their customs. They're not cold or calculating, and you will invariably come away from a number SIX feeling warm and uplifted. For this reason, they are truly loved and adored by their family, friends and associates. They are devoted to any task at hand and are fiercely loyal to loved ones, who adore them in return.

SIXES tend to be over-sentimental, which cannot be hidden or denied – it shows all over. This leads to a strong connection with their social standing, and how they present themselves to the community. Even if the bank is about to foreclose on them, they will remain tranquil and friendly. A SIX makes an ideal party guest, and you will always be assured of excellent entertainment, as he loves having friends and making others happy. SIXES enjoy expressing their natures through music, so you could find them singing on Broadway, or simply 'busking' in a subway. Discord and unpleasantness disturbs them, and they will do their utmost to settle disputes between people. They are the 'Grand Peacemakers' of the world.

The SIX person has a demanding side, which can emerge quite suddenly and catch you off guard. All of a sudden this gentle, sweet and cuddly person – whom you thought so charming – can flatten you with a stubbornness that is proportional to his generosity and kindness. Never mind; within minutes, the decorum will be restored and harmony will once again prevail.

SIXES attract money, be it through inheritance, work or marriage. But there could be a tendency towards extremes regarding money – they can be either very extravagant, or stingy to the point of being miserly. There is no neutral side to the finances of a SIX. Nevertheless, they will live in beautiful surroundings, as they love luxury and the sense of power it gives them. They will invariably drive the best of motorcars, even if it is ten or fifteen years old.

SIXES have impeccable manners and they dislike loud or rude people. Ugliness of any kind is distasteful to them. However, SIXES love to argue any point – if they believe they are right – but they prefer to do it with logic rather than passion. Logic usually wins, and passion could make them lose composure and destroy the romanticism of their persona. In such instances, they like to see themselves as the stoic hero in some great, fantastical Greek Drama (Heroes always win!). Failing this, they will convince you of their argument using their charm and sentimentality. You are sure to succumb sooner or later, because when they use this trick, they are so irresistible.

SEVEN — THE DIGNIFIED

Seven is associated with the element 'water'.
Seven is a passive processing number.

ACTIVE	REACTIVE
quiet	revengeful
conservative	reclusive
devoted	aloof
art lover	unemotional
detached	radical
dependable	temperamental
committed	intense
ambitious	anxious
refined	expressionless
inquiring	cautious
idealistic	controlling
	shy

Number SEVENS are all about water. That is their Element. To begin to understand them, think of an iceberg – most of it is hidden underwater, and you cannot see all of it unless you dive really deep.

SEVENS have a genuine 'aura' of power and dignity that other people sense, and their mere presence has a magnetic attraction. They are born leaders, especially in the field of theology and entertainment, and never follow the well-beaten track, but choose the path less travelled. SEVENS also have a wonderfully calming effect on others, but tend to bear burdens that do not belong to them. They hold onto other peoples' problems, and can become physically ill if they cannot deal with a specific struggle or problem. Like Atlas, they have a tendency to carry the world on their shoulders (this is similar to the WATER traits of a number TWO).

SEVENS have an inherent fear of the future, which is due to their insecurity. Often the only solution they can find for this anxiety is to accumulate money and material wealth. Even the most impoverished SEVEN will have something stashed away for a rainy day. They are also very cautious, and are not often drawn to speculation and chance. In spite of this need for material possessions, SEVENS have no fondness for wealth or material things – they are merely necessary to comfort their anxieties, and to give them room to contemplate the things that are important in life.

Number SEVENS are creative in many fields, be it advertising, acting, media, painting, sculpture, or dance. They have great skills in finance, but they could find this field rather limiting when it is done only for the sake of money. But this skill can prove very lucrative when combined with the creative powers of the SEVEN.

SEVENS need to 'be out and about' but, conversely, are also very private people. Do not try to pry into their private affairs, for they will simply avoid either you or the issue – or both, if necessary. SEVENS have a horror that their privacy may be invaded, and literally shudder at the thought. It's not that they have anything to hide – it's just that the things most people consider commonplace and not worth concealing, are often sacred to a number SEVEN – so don't go snooping around in their private belongings. They have ambitions that they will not discuss with others – you will simply see them suddenly emerge one day.

You would be amazed at the thoughts that swirl through the head of a SEVEN. They will never show this of course – the only thing you will get is the inevitable number SEVEN 'blank look'. It can take a long time before they trust people, and you will have to earn their trust by proving that you are not judgmental.

SEVENS will always find ways of improving their careers and lifestyles, and become very emotional during romance, which they take very seriously. Yet SEVENS play hard-to-get and their sensitivity is kept secret. When a partner makes a move, they retreat to a place of safety and expect you to come after them – so one needs to be persistent. Nevertheless, if the right person comes along, and who has the correct key to their emotions, they will open up and gush with enthusiasm. Until then, they will maintain that blank, disinterested look on their face – a typical 'matter of fact', bored look for which the SEVEN is well known.

Eight — Dependable

Eight is associated with the element 'earth'.
Eight is a dominant processing number.

ACTIVE	REACTIVE
stability	insecure
patient	intense
supportive	obsessive
experienced	undemonstrative
worldly-wise	calculating
responsible	overbearing
likes security	manipulative
serious	immovable
diligent	feels victimized
nonchalant	tends to play the sacrificial lamb

EIGHT is the number of ending and completion, and so number EIGHT people believe that tasks must be accomplished, no matter what obstacles are faced. EIGHTS are slow to anger, caring, methodical, and have infinite patience. They are generally quiet, reserved or even shy, and are not obvious in their movements and mannerisms. Slowly but surely, they will get to the end of whatever they are doing, and nothing will stop them. This can make EIGHTS rather immovable – not for the sake of being difficult, but for the sake of 'the task at hand'. This determination results in a burning ambition, and their shyness is usually a cover up for their intense desire to reach the top.

As children, many EIGHTS tend to have delicate constitutions. This creates insecurity, and accentuates the deep-seated fear that EIGHTS have of loss – so they need a lot of tender loving care. Their childhood insecurity is usually quite obvious and if a sensitive parent attends to it, the number EIGHT child is sure to blossom into a robust adult where longevity is very common, and who often get younger looking as they grow older.

EIGHTS also have a very subtle sense of humour – so listen carefully, or you could become the brunt of many a private joke. EIGHTS do not like to waste their spare time and like to be very productive, which often finds them indulging in a plethora of sports or hobbies. As they like to keep busy, and have a well-developed sense of duty, they can be relied upon to complete any task. But because they are so reliable, people tend to turn to EIGHTS for support – especially when they need to unload their emotional 'baggage' and have a shoulder to cry on. EIGHTS are the comforters of the needy.

EIGHTS don't appear to accept compliments, but secretly they love being told they are wonderful or efficient. They pretend to be the proverbial 'Rock of Gibraltar' – to show others that they are not weak. Any show of weakness is unthinkable for a number EIGHT, and for this reason they develop a remarkably deep, inner strength over the years. They can tend to become embroiled in other peoples' dramas by playing the role of supporter, and many times becoming the 'Instrument of Fate' for those people.

There is a tendency towards fanaticism in religion for EIGHTS and they will stick to what they believe in, at all costs. They are excellent people to have as friends, but can make formidable enemies. EIGHTS are also lonely people who crave love. For this reason, they do not demonstrate their affections easily – as they fear rejection – and would rather be alone with their own feelings, than get involved. EIGHTS are capable of great sacrifices, in the name of idealism and ambition. They have a love of nature, and can often be found in the country, or in a garden.

EIGHTS are as demanding of themselves as they are of others, and one of their lessons in life is to learn to be happy. They measure success by education, believing academic qualifications are the keys to wealth. EIGHTS enjoy corporate environments and will display an undying loyalty to their company – sticking with them through thick and thin – but the top position will always be in their sights. Although the ambitions of EIGHTS are often fulfilled in the business world, they also make good teachers, counsellors, doctors, vets and politicians. Anything that involves intelligent reasoning like crime detection, writing and science will also appeal to EIGHTS. They are often art lovers and enjoy expressing their views on the subject, or organising groups and societies dedicated to their passion.

NINE — THE CHILD

Nine has no element associated with it.
Nine is neither a dominant nor passive processing number.

ACTIVE	REACTIVE
unique	contradictory
naïve	confused
artistic	foolish
determined	impulsive
perceptive	forgetful
vulnerable	vain
innocent	lacks confidence
forgiving	stubborn
child-like	vague
honest	impatient

Number NINE people display wonderful child-like qualities having innocent, naïve and trusting natures. This often leads them into trouble with financial and business arrangements, where they can easily be taken for a ride. Usually, the number NINE will have to learn the hard way, unless they learn to follow their 'gut instincts', and let their powerful intuition become their guide.

One of the most beneficial talents of the number NINE, is an ability to penetrate right to core of a problem or situation. This alleviates the slow process of analysis, but due to this quickness of mind, NINES often become impatient with slower-thinking people. This doesn't help them in the popularity stakes as they can become so intolerant of mistakes that they become dramatic.

'What you see is what you get' best describes a number NINE. They do not know how to camouflage their emotions, and tend to blurt things out – even if it hurts. (Besides, it probably is the truth – and the truth can hurt!) For this reason they cannot – and do not – play emotional games with people. This gets NINES into a fix from time to time – innocently, of course. They are very vulnerable, and can become the victims of scheming or manipulative people, but if you tell them this, they will deny it vehemently.

Many people are touched by the child-like innocence and vulnerability of a NINE, and feel protective towards them. Others find them foolish or silly, and for this reason, working colleagues often don't respect them. Yet, when they spring into action, they surprise everyone with their courage and determination.

NINES have a deep-seated fear of rejection, which they do not handle easily. Even though they may seem self-assured, they constantly need reassurance. They need to hear that they are loved – or at least liked, respected or admired. They may seem cocky, very sure of themselves, and radiate an air of independence, but deep down inside they are very insecure and lack self-assurance. This is quite understandable when you remember that the number NINE is imbued with all the energies of the other numbers – so you can imagine the confusion that this creates from time to time.

Number NINES can be generous to a fault if they are in the mood, and their inherent instincts are to give and to help. They do not hold grudges and are usually very forgiving. This is why we often associate the number NINE with healing, be it alternative or allopathic. They are excellent at anything they put their mind to, be it medicine, law, travel, art, psychology, writing, designing, selling, investigating or simply standing up on a soap box preaching philosophy.

NINES have the ability to speak 'off the cuff', and you can always identify them by the way they speak, as they use spoonerisms. If you ask a number NINE for directions, a typical reply could be "As the fly crows!" They also seem to get confused about places, dates and names: "While I'm in New York, I'm going to the top of the Eiffel Tower". They mean the Empire State Building of course, but they speak what they picture in their mind's eye, and the words are irrelevant – you just have to work it out! A number NINE will love what they are doing, for as long as it takes their fancy. When they have had enough, they will simply get up and leave, to find something that interests them more. Perhaps one can describe them as 'A Jack of All Trades, and a Master of Most'.

HUMAN PIN CODE

INDIVIDUAL ANALYSIS

Birth date:_____

Male/Female (delete one)

	Elements	Dominant	Passive
Air			
Water		N/A	
Fire			N/A
Earth	N/A		
Nine	N/A		

LIFE STAGE MATRIX
ON REVERSE

Life cycle:									
Nursery	0	1	2	3	4	5	6	7	8
Year:									
Teenage	9	10	11	12	13	14	15	16	17
Bachelor	18	19	20	21	22	23	24	25	26
Nesting	27	28	29	30	31	32	33	34	35
Adulthood	36	37	38	39	40	41	42	43	44
Spiritual	45	46	47	48	49	50	51	52	53
Family	54	55	56	57	58	59	60	61	62
Achievement	63	64	65	66	67	68	69	70	71
Wisdom	72	And onwards							

HUMAN PIN CODE

INDIVIDUAL ANALYSIS

Birth date:_____

Male/Female (delete one)

	Elements	Dominant	Passive
Air			
Water		N/A	
Fire			N/A
Earth	N/A		
Nine	N/A		

LIFE STAGE MATRIX
ON REVERSE

Life cycle: Nursery Year:	0	1	2	3	4	5	6	7	8
Teenage	9	10	11	12	13	14	15	16	17
Bachelor	18	19	20	21	22	23	24	25	26
Nesting	27	28	29	30	31	32	33	34	35
Adulthood	36	37	38	39	40	41	42	43	44
Spiritual	45	46	47	48	49	50	51	52	53
Family	54	55	56	57	58	59	60	61	62
Achievement	63	64	65	66	67	68	69	70	71
Wisdom	72	And onwards							

Human Pin Code

Individual Analysis

Birth date:_____

Male/Female (delete one)

	Elements	Dominant	Passive
Air			
Water		N/A	
Fire			N/A
Earth	N/A		
Nine	N/A		

Life Stage Matrix
on reverse

Life cycle: Nursery Year:	0	1	2	3	4	5	6	7	8
Teenage	9	10	11	12	13	14	15	16	17
Bachelor	18	19	20	21	22	23	24	25	26
Nesting	27	28	29	30	31	32	33	34	35
Adulthood	36	37	38	39	40	41	42	43	44
Spiritual	45	46	47	48	49	50	51	52	53
Family	54	55	56	57	58	59	60	61	62
Achievement	63	64	65	66	67	68	69	70	71
Wisdom	72	And onwards							

HUMAN PIN CODE

INDIVIDUAL ANALYSIS

Birth date:_____

Male/Female (delete one)

	Elements	Dominant	Passive
Air			
Water		N/A	
Fire			N/A
Earth	N/A		
Nine	N/A		

LIFE STAGE MATRIX
ON REVERSE

Life cycle:									
Nursery	0	1	2	3	4	5	6	7	8
Year:									
Teenage	9	10	11	12	13	14	15	16	17
Bachelor	18	19	20	21	22	23	24	25	26
Nesting	27	28	29	30	31	32	33	34	35
Adulthood	36	37	38	39	40	41	42	43	44
Spiritual	45	46	47	48	49	50	51	52	53
Family	54	55	56	57	58	59	60	61	62
Achievement	63	64	65	66	67	68	69	70	71
Wisdom	72	And onwards							

HUMAN PIN CODE
SYNERGY CALCULATION

Birth date: _____   Birth date: _____

Male / Female (delete one)   Male / Female (delete one)

Elements	Dominant	Passive		Elements	Dominant	Passive
			Air			
	N/A		Water		N/A	
		N/A	Fire			N/A
			Earth			
N/A			Nine	N/A		
N/A			Total	N/A		

_____ Dominant / Passive   _____ Dominant / Passive
(delete as neccessary)   (delete as neccessary)

Synergy Pin Code

	Elements	Dominant	Passive
Air			
Water		N/A	
Fire			N/A
Earth			
Nine	N/A		
Total	N/A		

_____ Dominant / Passive (delete as neccessary)

Human Pin Code
Synergy Calculation

Birth date: _____

Male / Female (delete one)

Birth date: _____

Male / Female (delete one)

Elements	Dominant	Passive		Elements	Dominant	Passive
			Air			
	N/A		Water		N/A	
		N/A	Fire			N/A
			Earth			
N/A			Nine	N/A		
N/A			Total	N/A		

_____ Dominant / Passive
(delete as neccessary)

_____ Dominant / Passive
(delete as neccessary)

Synergy Pin Code

	Elements	Dominant	Passive
Air			
Water		N/A	
Fire			N/A
Earth			
Nine	N/A		
Total	N/A		

_____ Dominant / Passive (delete as neccessary)

Human Pin Code
Synergy Calculation

Birth date: _____

Male / Female (delete one)

Birth date: _____

Male / Female (delete one)

Elements	Dominant	Passive		Elements	Dominant	Passive
			Air			
	N/A		Water		N/A	
		N/A	Fire			N/A
			Earth			
N/A			Nine	N/A		
N/A			Total	N/A		

_____ Dominant / Passive
(delete as neccessary)

_____ Dominant / Passive
(delete as neccessary)

Synergy Pin Code

	Elements	Dominant	Passive
Air			
Water		N/A	
Fire			N/A
Earth			
Nine	N/A		
Total	N/A		

_____ Dominant / Passive (delete as neccessary)

Human Pin Code
Synergy Calculation

Birth date: _____

Male / Female (delete one)

Birth date: _____

Male / Female (delete one)

Elements	Dominant	Passive		Elements	Dominant	Passive
			Air			
	N/A		Water		N/A	
		N/A	Fire			N/A
			Earth			
N/A			Nine	N/A		
N/A			Total	N/A		

_____ Dominant / Passive
(delete as neccessary)

_____ Dominant / Passive
(delete as neccessary)

Synergy Pin Code

	Elements	Dominant	Passive
Air			
Water		N/A	
Fire			N/A
Earth			
Nine	N/A		
Total	N/A		

_____ Dominant / Passive (delete as neccessary)

Practitioner and consultant information

Since the creation of the Human Pin Code formulae, its application has spread widely. This book has been written for readers to gain a basic understanding of how the formulae are used and can be applied for individual Pin Code readings and Synergy Pin Code readings. The book teaches you to apply the formulae and to do basic analyses. It's simple enough for you to then practise using the formulae on your own birth date and those of your family and friends.

To ensure the integrity of the Human Pin Code and to encourage the precise application of the formulae, a certification course has been established for people who are interested in using the Human Pin Code to provide professional analyses and readings for others.

It is strongly recommended that anyone interested in obtaining a professional analysis or reading, or in attending classes or workshops, to only approach an *officially certified Human Pin Code practitioner* as the accuracy of information provided by uncertified practitioners cannot be guaranteed.

The purchase of this book does not qualify the reader to undertake professional Human Pin Code analyses. If anyone wishes to notify Douglas Forbes of an uncertified person conducting analyses for financial gain, please do so at info@humanpincode.com. Douglas does not endorse any uncertified person who is doing such work without a license and reserves the right to seek damages as he sees fit.

Information on certified practitioners, certification, personal readings and workshops can be found at www.humanpincode.com or please contact the Human Pin Code office on +27 11 487 0984 or email info@humanpincode.com.

Corporate Services

Companies in South Africa are already making use of the scientific analysis in the Human Pin Code to improve their productivity amongst employees.

The services that are offered are in the areas of:

• Human Resources

• Profiling

• Team Building

• Conflict Resolution

If you are representing a corporate entity, you too can use the Human Pin Code in your organisation. Please contact us with your request at info@humanpincode.com or call the Human Pin Code office on +27 11 487 0984